ragged run

A Memoir of Survival

BARNABY DINGES

www.mascotbooks.com

Ragged Run

©2019 Barnaby Dinges. All Rights Reserved. No part of this publication may be reproduced, stored in a retrieval system or transmitted in any form by any means electronic, mechanical, or photocopying, recording or otherwise without the permission of the author.

Some names and identifying details have been changed to protect the privacy of individuals.

I have tried to recreate events, locales, and conversations from my memories of them. In order to maintain their anonymity, in some instances I have changed the names of individuals and places. I may have changed some identifying characteristics and details such as physical properties, occupations, and places of residence.

For more information, please contact:
Mascot Books
620 Herndon Parkway #320
Herndon, VA 20170
info@mascotbooks.com

Book design by Ricky Frame

Library of Congress Control Number: 2019902498

CPSIA Code: PRFRE0419A
ISBN-13: 978-1-64307-440-5

Printed in Canada

To Vicky,
for showing me what
happiness feels like.

Rag-ged

Adjective

1. Having an irregular
   edge or outline

2. Torn or worn to tatters;
   worn out from stress and
   strain ("ran herself ragged")

3. Wearing tattered clothes

prologue

It took the pain of going through a divorce at age 40 to get me into therapy. I should have gone sooner, but I was too busy functioning at just high enough a level to have a family and maintain a lucrative public relations job in Chicago. I was raising two sons: Cooper, eight, and Hayden, six. Having them grow up in a household with a mom and dad gave me tremendous joy; I was watching the childhood I'd hoped for my older brother and me.

Divorce ravages the souls of most people who go through it, but in my case, it felt debilitating—like absorbing a death with each new day. It felt like the biggest loss of my life. But there had been other losses, much bigger, that had happened more than 30 years earlier, in the late 1960s.

Over those three decades, I'd found a way to function, to excel in college, make lifelong friends, fall in love, have kids, and enjoy successful careers in teaching, politics, and public relations. I saw the world in black and white, and I lived with a limited range of emotion, mostly hilarity or rage. But I wanted more. I wanted to experience the world in living color, to feel and share the full range of human emotion. I knew there was more of me to share, but it was buried inside.

My therapist suggested I try writing a letter to my nine-year-old self and forgive him for what happened. Tell him he was not to blame. He was there, but HE DIDN'T DO IT! It was not his fault. He was in the room, but HE WASN'T RESPONSIBLE! I figured, *why not give it a shot?* I was 40 and still had half my life to live. If you're going through the burning tunnel of divorce, why not burn off a few other life warts at the same time?

I wrote the "Dear Barnaby" letter and then read it to my

therapist the next time I saw him. He complimented me on my honesty and asked me how I felt.

"I feel dead," I said.

He told me to let it sink in. Maybe read it again to myself in the near future.

I left the therapist's office in downtown Chicago and headed to the El train on one of those humid Midwest summer days, when a river of sweat forms down your back the instant you step outdoors. The El was packed, and to distract myself from discomfort, I pulled out the letter and read the words silently. When I got to the end, tears started to roll down my cheeks. Not just a few tears. A flow of tears so uncontrolled they were rolling off my chin and landing on my dress shirt, forming two large wet spots on my chest.

I put on my aviator sunglasses to hide my tears from the fellow commuters packed all around me. But the tears kept coming, in waves. A young woman stood facing me less than a foot away. I worried that my tears were bouncing off my chest and onto her.

She looked intently up at me and asked sweetly, "Sir, is everything all right? Are you okay?"

After a pause to gather myself, I responded, "My parents just died."

That's how it felt at that moment. I'd waited 31 years to let myself experience it. In the course of an hour, it became devastatingly real and the gaping hole of losing my parents crashed right through me.

And with that moment, a flood of memories became vivid; reflections of a ragged run through a sad childhood that would shape the man I became.

part
one

1962

IT ALL STARTED OFF SCARY, not sad at all.

I awoke in this world when a loud truck horn blared outside the cabin. The sound was so loud it scared me out of bed, and I fell to the floor. It was getting light outside. I wanted to get back into bed, so I reached up, but I could barely touch the edge of the mattress—too small to climb back into my bed.

The cabin was now silent, and all I could see were dust balls on the dark brown wooden floors. Slow and silent, I walked around the seemingly vast cabin but saw no one. Where were my parents? Did I even have parents? Is this what it would feel like to be alone in the world?

Then, along a two-story A-frame wall of long horizontal beams, I saw a ladder leading up to a hole cut into the wall. It was a man-made ladder, unsteady and not sturdy, but it invited me to climb. I didn't know I could.

I climbed slowly up a dozen or so steps as if into a tree house and peered inside the dark hole into a small room. Through the darkness, on a small mattress on the floor, I saw a boy about five sleeping. It was my brother, Casey. I crawled over and lay beside him, and I must have fallen back to sleep, because that's all I remember about that.

I was three years old, and we were staying at the old Dinges family cabin in Port Elgin, Canada, just north of Michigan.

1963

WE LIVED IN A TYPICAL Chicago "three-flat" with a vestibule entrance, a living room off to the right, a long hallway with three bedrooms on each side, a dining room with a side room that contained a couch and a TV, and a pantry leading into a kitchen at the back of the apartment. There was a small room off the kitchen for storage where my Granny would stay the few times she visited.

We lived on the first of three floors in a yellow-brick building off an alley, with a Christian Science Church on the other side of the alley that featured big stained glass windows. We had a basement, which had a washer and dryer and room for storage. A few steps up was our back porch and an asphalt jungle of a backyard, and there was a small strip of grass between our three-flat and the one to the west. Though that shaded piece of grass was only 15 feet by 100, my brother and I used it for playing football on what felt like a regulation-sized field.

Ricka

I liked to sit on the floor in the kitchen looking up at my mother. My mom was a joy to observe, always wearing something stylish and colorful that the model Twiggy might look good in, moving around the kitchen. She didn't like to cook much, and she wasn't very good at it. She hated to clean, and she did the job so casually that my dad would always rinse out a coffee cup before using it, figuring it was either unclean or still soapy. I could watch my mom do anything, and I did. We had a TV, but I would only watch it if my mom made me a peanut butter and jelly sandwich and a glass of milk and guided me into the dining room to lie on the floor and watch *Bozo's Circus*.

My mom liked to drink coffee, smoke cigarettes, and talk on the phone. Sometimes she would do all three at one time, propping open the window off the pantry a few inches, just enough to sneak an ashtray onto the window sill. She would pull a chair over and sit overlooking the alley, taking advantage of the ten-foot extension cord of the wall-mounted phone. I listened to her laughing, or getting angry, sometimes crying ... and always swearing. She was good at it. She used cuss words like punctuation.

My mom's name was Ricka, and she was classy. Her name had been Marie Claire Leonhardt when she and her parents fled the Nazis from Danzig, Germany in 1938 when she was seven years old. According to family lore, as she learned English as a young girl, she struggled to say "America" and it came out more like "AmeRicka." So, Ricka became her name. (Cool names were valued in our family. My dad, Charles Vern Dinges III, was known as Chuck. My brother, Charles Vern Dinges IV, was Casey. And I got branded with the funkiest name of all—Barnaby Leonhardt Dinges. My parents gave me the heart of a lion, and the name to prove it.)

Ricka liked to write. She wrote letters, mostly to college friends and her mother. She wrote in her journal often, and she wrote essays for *Vogue* about trying to do and have it all ... long before anyone had any useful advice about any of that.

She worked on a manual typewriter, a baby-blue and white Smith Corona, positioned atop a desk by the front window in her home. She wrote with her back to the street, looking down the long hallway into the apartment, which was empty because my brother was at school and my dad was at work.

I would position myself on the floor below the desk, between her legs, looking in the same direction she did. We didn't talk. She would write, and I would play with little metal cars and plastic soldiers. I would hear the clatter of her fast typing above. What a wonderful rhythm. What a peaceful place. What a happy time. What a perfect home.

I knew Mom kept a journal, because in 1978, during my freshman year at college when I was home for winter break, I found it. At the urging of my financial advisor (who questioned the $30-a-month fee to rent the storage space), I was rummaging through a bunch of boxes full of my parents' possessions in a cold dark warehouse in the north end of the city, I found her writings in a wicker basket. The writing was mostly in blue-ink calligraphy, but there were also many typed pages and even carbon copies of some letters she had sent to friends and her mother. She wrote in a dramatic way, as if she knew she would be read some day by others. Finding her journal among boxes of mostly junk, was jarring. After not seeing her or hearing her voice for more than ten years, it was as if she were speaking again ... and I was listening.

She described her journal like this:

> *I have kept a journal in an attempt to remain sane because I could not believe what was going on. I had hoped to capture some of the quality of this time and place in the day-to-day workings of one of its ordinary (uneminent) members. For it is said that just as eminent figures qualified the Victorian period, so our age is characterized by its mass men. And if I fail, I hope the very character of failure might somehow be revealing ... I am an aging sorority girl, in short, probably entirely*

too shrill, who can say only in her own defense that she·
was interested, even if no one else was. I have the dark
hope that my notes, now in themselves incredibly trivial,
might by that very nature, in the sufficient passage of
time, become positively fascinating ... I hope to have
been trivial in an indicative way.

Chuck

My dad, Chuck, would arrive home from work, usually after dark, and we would greet him in the vestibule. He would take off his hat and open his trench coat to let the three of us dive in for a raucous hug. I could smell the soothing manly mix of cologne and sweat from a long day working downtown.

My dad was a rising creative director at a small but booming Chicago advertising firm, which was creating catchy campaigns for products that were all taking off in the early 1960s. The competition was fierce, but my dad seemed to love the challenge. Out of his head and through his gifted hands came great ad concepts for emerging brands such as Old Milwaukee beer ("Have one. Have Another. It's that Kind of Beer"); Belair cigarettes ("Belair. The taste that's got the light touch of menthol. And Raleigh coupons, too"); and Old Thompson whiskey ("People who pay less, often know more"). Heady stuff for a 32-year-old graphic artist just a decade out of college. The ads depicted attractive, well-dressed young people having a good time, just like Ricka and Chuck. They were a 1960s couple who sported about in a black Corvair, listened to the Beatles, and loved JFK (especially Mom). Their idea of a fun Saturday night was to invite a few couples over, roll out the Ping-Pong table in the dining room, fire up the phonograph, and drink and smoke and play until late into the night.

My dad loved 16-inch softball. He was the star switch-hitting shortstop on the company team, which played in a league of advertising firms that took over Grant Park south of downtown Chicago one night per week during the warm summers. It was memorable because my dad, normally reserved around his more social and vocal wife, became an energized animal at these games. He shouted at teammates, ran all around the diamond, and tended to get his shiny blue uniform very dirty.

One day, a Chicago police officer invited me to hop aboard his three-wheeled vehicle for a drive around the park. I absolutely loved the ride until I realized I had been so lost in the journey that I got a big burn on my inner thigh from the hot pipes of the machine. My cries of pain ruined the family picnic, and I'm not sure I was ever invited back.

It didn't matter, though, because my dad stopped playing not long after that. I remember after one game, Dad came home and I saw him lying in bed, still in his shiny blue uniform and looking totally drained and defeated. He stayed there for a few days. Mom told Casey and me not to bother him; he wasn't feeling well. After that, Chuck started to lose hair and weight. He still looked good, but probably about ten years older than he was. I didn't think anything of it. I figured he was working his tail off downtown and taking over the advertising industry one drawing at a time.

Mom wrote:

Charles, Chuck, Bud, Buddy Hey Dinges, MISTER Dinges. Honored group leader. Chuck is the way he likes to be—harried, over worked, driven, bugged, exhausted. He has his worries, and he worries over them faithfully and with, let the record show, a high degree

of success. He did it with a pencil. He draws pictures.
Or rather did. He drew so well he no longer draws.
Now he writes. I want it explained to me. I asked him
once what he did for a living, and he said he was paid
to go to meetings and say NO. I could allege this has
colored his lifestyle. The gentle artist I married, recently
turned into a management manipulator, quite capable
of COMING HOME and saying no. And with some
heat and conviction. Chuck is pretty well right now.
The motorcycle season is coming. He really likes adver-
tising, family life, sports, and his motorcycle. Known to
others as the Death Machine. His other great interest is
… ugliness. He likes bizarrerie—his whole mind may
be what is now called "camp." He likes the outrageous
and macabre, the appalling—it sort of cheers him up.

Bikes

My dad bought a sleek little white Honda motorcycle—a
Dream 150 that could top out at 70 mph. He would park the bike
diagonally in front of our first-floor apartment on Wrightwood
Avenue in the heart of Chicago's Lincoln Park neighborhood. It
was an emerging middle-class neighborhood in the 1960s, stocked
with old three-flats that were perfect for aspiring families like ours.

I would watch Dad climb on his motorcycle from the front
window and jet off without a helmet and in full work attire for the
ten-minute ride to the Palmolive Building, which was Chicago's
first skyscraper—a 33-floor art deco wonder that had a beacon on
top that shone out over Lake Michigan to help boats and airplanes
find their way to and around Chicago's growing metro area.

On weekends, Dad would load Casey and me on to the Honda: my brother in back holding the strap on the seat, and me wedged in the middle holding on to my dad for dear life. The ride to the White Castle burger joint on Addison and Ashland was not long, but it seemed like an eternity because I never felt stable or secure on the bike. Though my dad was only 5'7" and 130 pounds, I could never really get my arms around his waist. Behind me, Casey had his own issues holding on and keeping his heels from catching the spokes of the rear wheel. Pants-crappingly scary as the journey was, when we got to White Castle (and I believed it to be a REAL castle), the onion-steamed sliders made the near-death experience worth it. I was hooked from the start and would beg Dad to risk our lives for those tasty burgers every Saturday.

One evening, we had an early dinner, just the four of us. We were eating in the dining room, which made it feel a little special. Mom and Dad were sitting across from each other talking about their day, and Casey and I were making faces at each other while we ate. During dinner there was a rustle on the back porch, and my dad jumped up from the table and ran to the kitchen to see out of the back window. There he saw two young boys heading out of the alley with his and Mom's bikes. He ran out onto the porch, but by that time, the thieves were well on their way. (We kept our bikes on the back porch, making it easy to get them down to the alley and out on the street and to the park a minute away.) "Motherfucking Puerto Rican bike stealers!" my dad yelled down the alley after them. At that moment, and for several years afterward, I thought that only Puerto Ricans stole bikes.

Turtles

I also recall that though we were not much of a pet family, at some point we took on a rescue dog—an adult standard poodle named Sugar. She seemed nice enough, but she had trouble adjusting to apartment living ... at least our apartment. One evening, we went out and left Sugar enclosed in the long hallway that ran from the vestibule entrance to the living room. It was about 40 feet long and five feet wide, but when all the doors were shut, she was left in a long dark room. We came home to discover she had crapped along the entire length of the hallway, including up the walls. That night I heard cuss words from my dad's mouth I had never heard before.

A week later, we took Sugar for a family walk to enjoy the evening air in Lincoln Park and have my brother, Casey, learn how to walk the dog on a leash. But Sugar saw a squirrel and dragged Casey down the sidewalk for an entire city block. His body and clothes were torn up from the pavement encounter. Then, one day, Sugar disappeared from the apartment without a word of explanation.

Later, we got three turtles, and they lived in a small, windowed box in my room. They lived atop a large low-lying table that my mom had painted in paisley swirls of browns and white in kind of a racetrack formation that I would use with my toy cars. One weekend, I was playing in my room, and I felt sorry for the three little turtles because they were stuck in their box. I thought they might want to go for a swim in the bathroom sink. One at a time, I grabbed them and put them into the sink and put the stopper in to hold the water. The sink had two faucets, and I must have turned on the hot one first because it came out steaming. I peered over the edge of the sink in horror. They were floating upside down.

Just then, my dad came into the bathroom, and seeing the

three cooked creatures, picked me up without a word, walked over to my bed, flipped me over and gave my rump the only spanking he would ever deliver. It hurt, and I cried, but I knew I deserved it. What struck me was the swiftness with which my dad delivered my punishment. Yes, I'd done a terrible thing … but I think it was that I showed him something he didn't need to see. DEATH.

1964

Christmas

My parents were committed to treating their sons as equals to the point of dressing us in similar outfits, like twins. On Christmas Eve, Mom and Dad had piled up what looked to be two identical pyramids of presents side by side on the living room floor. While all the gifts were not the same, once stacked they looked alike. My brother would get a baseball and some trading cards, and I would get a few Corgi die-cast cars. I wasn't quite ready for the big leagues.

We each raced through our gift piles and got to the bottom to find a large cork board to hang in our rooms, complete with the aluminum tacks Dad used at his office to hang creative concepts and pictures on the wall. (A trip to Dad's office was a treat because it would be on a Saturday morning, riding the Honda along the lakefront to the majestic Palmolive Building. Dad's office had thick paper, glue, and colored pens; the chemical smell off those pens gave me quite the adolescent buzz. The big thick markers were the best.) So, when we were gifted with the cork boards, that was a happy time because it would always make me think of my dad, downtown at work, creating bold images and ideas to sell products.

Casey and I got one gift to share that year: a new toy called Rock 'Em Sock 'Em Robots. I think my parents were sending us a subtle message ("Stop fighting all the time!"). The toy was a small yellow plastic boxing ring with two hulking robots, one blue and the other red. On the opposite side of the ring were two thumb controllers that could be depressed to cause the robots to throw punches. And, boy, could those robots throw down! The robots would pound away at each other for a few seconds before one of their heads would randomly pop up and make a screeching sound, ending the duel. Depressing the losing robot's head back into place meant another skirmish could begin. We could fight for hours, and we did.

Casey and I liked that toy so much that early the next morning, *real* Christmas Day, we went out into the hallway between our identical bedrooms to duke it out with the robots. After a short while, Dad emerged from the bedroom off the vestibule, casting a long shadow our way. "Knock it off and get back to bed!" he yelled, and we scurried back into our separate rooms and beds. I lay there, struck that Dad had been naked as he had screamed at us ... and his silhouette in the morning light made him appear rail thin.

Mom & Dad

Mom and Dad met at Michigan State University in East Lansing in 1949, when my mom was quite a catch. She was the only child of Hans Leonhardt and his British dancer wife, Doreen Seaton. The three had fled Germany in 1938, just as Hitler was closing in on Jewish professionals like my grandfather. (Hans was a maritime lawyer in the port city of Danzig who worked to free many Jewish families before he himself loaded up a few suitcases and left Germany for America.) Because Doreen was British, they were able to pack two suitcases of valuables and travel to London for a weekend "vacation" that would end up lasting a lifetime.

In America they settled in Lansing, where Hans taught International Politics and Doreen taught German and Russian languages at MSU. Hans wrote an influential book, *Nazi Conquest of Danzig*, and he traveled the country giving lectures on topics like the future of Europe, post-Hitler.

As she grew up, Ricka was known on campus for her stylish European flair and the fact that she was Hans Leonhardt's daughter. Hans intimidated the hell out of his students because he routinely challenged them for their complacency amid world turmoil and their lack of intellectual vigor.

I know from an old photograph that when Chuck showed up for a date with Ricka in college, he wore a baggy print shirt, wrinkled khaki pants, and scuffed white shoes, and his hair was slicked back James Dean style. Ricka wore a sensible sleeveless white top, a black skirt with a hemline below her knees, and black flats that resembled ballet slippers.

With my mother's style influence, Chuck went a long way from the starving-artist look in the 1950s to a dashing, Bond-like executive in the 1960s. The U.S. Army probably helped clean up his act, too. He was stationed in Biloxi, MS and El Paso, TX, although much of his time was spent in the company of a group of artists who filled their evenings with drawing and making music, artists including Robert Benton (who went on to create movies such as *Bonnie and Clyde*, *Kramer vs. Kramer*, and *Places in the Heart*) and Robert Massey, who would become an esteemed artist working in charcoal.

Dad must have loved the army crew cut because that became his go-to look in his early 30s, and he shared the joy with Casey and me. Mom and Dad would also make us wear saddle shoes— those black and white numbers that never looked good on anyone at any time. Once a year, they would dress us in ironed shorts, dress shirts, and sport coats and march us to a photographer who would take pictures of us in goofy fake poses on an old-fashioned bicycle. I'm not sure who they were trying to impress, or what airs they were trying to cast, but the black-and-white enlarged photos make ridiculous memories today.

Occasionally, my mom's style sense would break down. One time she sent me to nursery school wearing a beat-up pair of saddle shoes, long baggy hand-me-down pants rolled up with a five-inch cuff, and a loose long-sleeve shirt buttoned to the top. I looked like I was dressed in clothes from the Jimmy Hoffa fall collection. And with the crew cut, I might as well have been a prisoner standing around the yard wasting away the afternoon.

> *We are, as they say, well. That is to say we are tired, cross, temperamental, doubting, sulky and full of blasted ego ... Chuck is busy, he overworks with a kind of Slavic joy, cursing the work and never leaving it for a minute. Case and Bar are cooling at an excellent school, Francis W. Parker, of which accomplishment we are exceedingly vain. The school being so good that even my two progress. Case stands number one in first grade and runs evaporation experiments all over my window sills. He is our man for dinosaurs, magnets, hydrodynamics, and does a fair twist, interested in little beyond tangoes and study. Bar, our existentialist, is in junior kindergarten, whatever that is, manufacturing collage and social leverage and generally making himself felt. He is our actor—the corn in both families settled in his veins and clotted. He is social, agreeable, irrational, and has, as could be predicted, the ear for language. I say fuck 'em both ... I totter about at the fringe of "a career." I*

haven't time enough to really pursue it yet, but have too much time not to, and lead the bastard life of the unpublished author who is not even unpublished ... All this is burdened by the fact that it will be another three years before I have both my snerds in school full time, and so the grandeur must be chiseled in small fits and limpid starts. I am in bad humor and my health is not good.

School

The early 1960s were a time when automobiles had no seatbelts and parents let their young children take the bus alone to get to school. Casey and I attended the exclusive Francis W. Parker School (FWP) on the city's north side, right across from the Lincoln Park Zoo and just blocks from the beach and Lake Michigan. Tuition for kindergarten was $500 in 1963.

Founded in 1901 by Civil War veteran Col. Francis Wayland Parker, with help from benefactor Anita McCormick Blaine, the school became an innovator and leader in progressive education. Critical thinking, persuasive communication, and community service became the bedrock of the curriculum. When FWP built a new school in 1962 (at the cost of $2.2 million), ambitious parents like Chuck and Ricka Dinges flocked to place their kids at the Lincoln Park campus.

The city bus cost 12 cents for a child, and though the school was barely a half mile from our apartment, Casey was allowed to walk over to Stockton Avenue to catch the bus. So, for a quarter he could get to school and back, while I was subjected to a half day of school and carpooling with three girls in my class. I remember my brother, a dutiful first child, would count out the two dimes and four pennies he would need each day to get to and from to school. (This is the same kid who, when we were at a restaurant waiting for food, would take Dad's fine-point calligraphy pen and sketch an elaborate drawing of two football players colliding, accurate down to the uniform design and athletic position of the players at the point of impact.)

One afternoon, I was following Mom around the apartment when she answered the phone and broke into an immediate panic. She called Chuck at work, and then we raced to a nearby hospital. Casey had been in an accident. He'd suffered a head injury and was unconscious. Casey had been near the zoo, waiting for the bus with a classmate, when he realized that he lacked the 12 cents necessary to board. He dashed past the stopped bus on his way back to school to get his bus fare, but he ran into a through lane and got hit by a taxicab. Apparently, the Yellow Cab clipped him on the left side of his head, spinning him in the air. Eyewitnesses said he flew in the air about 20 feet before his face skidded on the ground and he landed in an unconscious heap in the middle of Stockton Drive.

Casey made a miraculous recovery, and two days later he was back at home. One side of his face was a huge brown-red scab which kept his right eye shut. My brother was a beautifully handsome boy. He looked like a young JFK, the president my mom adored, and to see Casey in such gruesome condition was hard. I remember that he stayed home from school a week more until his scab looked less monstrous. Mom and Dad seemed shaken by the incident. They dodged another bullet, but Casey, fast as he was, couldn't dodge that cab.

Play

While many of my friends would stay around after school to play baseball in the park, I liked to hit a construction site on the way home, and there were many. I enjoyed the ruggedness of the 1960s. This was a time when many of the three-flat apartments near the park were being torn down to make way for taller towers that would have views of the lake. I didn't care about that; what I liked was the work sites that were completely open and accessible. No chain-link fences to keep the riffraff out.

I would meet up with a few neighborhood kids, and we'd wait until midafternoon when the work crews would leave for the day. The best sites were the ones where demolition was still underway and building supplies were being stored for future use. We'd start by assisting in the demolition, usually breaking glass with bricks and looking through the rubble for treasures. When we got bored with that, we graduated to using the new bricks and wood to erect our own sculptures. Inevitably, the designs we built either fell over from poor engineering, or we'd bomb them with bricks until all that remained was a pile of debris, looking very much like the demolition piles. I'm sure the construction workers loved us when they arrived the next morning.

One day, we got a little carried away and lost track of time. Too much fun in the dirt pit. I was always supposed to be home before sundown, and I must have been fooled by those powerful Chicago street lights. Mayor Richard J. Daley sure knew how to light up his city. In the midst of building another architectural wonder, I was surprised by two police officers with flashlights, one asking, "Are you the Dinges kid?" I knew this was not going to end well, so I answered yes. "Your mom called us an hour ago, and we've been looking all over the neighborhood for you. Do you know your mom is having a dinner party tonight? You are in big trouble."

Though less than two blocks from home, it was the longest journey I'd experienced. When I entered the vestibule, my mom grabbed me by the wrist and walked me down the hallway and put me right into bed in my dirty clothes. No drink, no dinner, no goodnight kiss—which was a first. My days always ended with my mom tucking me in, looking down on me with her beautiful face, saying, "Sweet dreams Bar-Bar. I love you." But not this night. As I lay there looking at the ceiling, still in a daze, I could hear some loud chatter out in the dining room. They were probably talking about what a rotten kid I was. I didn't feel rotten. I was a kid who liked having fun.

A few minutes later my door opened and in came one of my mom's lady friends. I could hear the clink of ice in her glass as she put it on my table and came over to sit on the edge of my bed.

"Is my mom going to come and kiss me goodnight?" I asked.

As my mom's friend leaned in over me, I could smell the warmth of alcohol on her breath as she hovered close over me. She said, "Not tonight. Ricka is very upset. You scared her to death. But everything will be all right in the morning."

With that, she slowly turned, grabbed her drink, and left. And I learned my first life lesson. Every tomorrow is a new day; a shitty today can still be a great tomorrow.

1965

I'M NOT CERTAIN WHEN I first learned that I was small. Really small. By first grade, I was the shortest kid in my class, girls included, by a good half a head. But it didn't bother me unless someone pointed it out. I remember a doctor's appointment when they weighed and measured me: 48 inches tall and 48 pounds. The world seemed in perfect balance. Or at least I did.

My caring kindergarten grade teacher, Peggy Nesbitt, described me this way:

> *Barnaby is a dear little boy who tries desperately to keep the fact of his small size from becoming an important factor in his life. He succeeds in proving this to his peers by playing rough, trying everything that comes his way, and succeeding in almost everything physical that he endeavors to do. He is fast moving and beautifully coordinated.*
>
> *Quite a likable fellow, Barnaby often finds himself in the role of leader because of his varied and imaginative ideas. He much prefers active, physical play, but much to his surprise, finds himself enjoying the doll corner, rhythms, and music. He learned words to songs quickly and easily.*
>
> *Barnaby has a natural flair for artwork. His ideas do not seem to be premeditated, but he conceives things as he*

works. In a few moments he has created something beautiful and relative to his experiences. He works quickly and effortlessly, and the product is usually something to be proud of.

Although quite competent in oral discourse, Barnaby seems quite self-conscious when speaking before the group and often resorts to clowning and pre-fabrication. He speaks rapidly and occasionally stammers as a result. Despite this, he desires to participate regularly in Show & Tell period. We have tried to make him feel as comfortable as possible to help him see that his stories are interesting without the added embellishments.

We believe that his loud and often boisterous voice is another outlet for expression of strength and position.

Being small was just flat-out cool. Being short and quick made me hard to tag in touch football games during recess at school. Girls thought I was cute, maybe a little less brutish than the big oafs in the class. And being low to the ground, I could scoop up coins and other valuables that were strewn about.

Smallness made me want to perform: first to prove myself, and then to entertain others. Early on, I must have realized that my dad was sick and my mom was suffering, and so I needed to find a way to make them feel better. If I could make them laugh, maybe it would take their minds off the tragedy that was coming, even momentarily. My purpose in life was to be the court jester and to pop the bubble of gloom.

I don't remember many days spent with my dad. I do recall that on Saturdays he used to like to walk Casey and me east a few blocks into Lincoln Park to play soccer. Dad had a friend from the advertising world named Brendan Nolan, a dashing Brit with a thick London accent and a tolerance for spending time with kids. He was single at the time. A few years later he would meet a sweet stewardess on a United Airlines flight, Christine from Cleveland, and they would ultimately marry and move back to London to raise three boys of their own. Two of them, Christopher and Jonathan Nolan, would become famous for making movies.

Brendan would bring his soccer ball, and we would play two on two on the lawn in front of the Alexander Hamilton statue. The lawn was perhaps 20 yards by 40, but it felt like a full-sized pitch back then. I liked soccer because the ball was right there on the ground and being close to it was a plus; speed and maneuverability were advantages. I'd found my game. I don't recall ever getting tired. Run. Run. Run.

We sometimes fantasize that our parents are great at everything they do. At some point as an adult, while going through family photos, I saw some pictures of my dad in an English riding cap and holding a three-wood golf club, down at the driving range a few blocks from our apartment—the Diversey Driving range off Lake Shore Drive—where he worked on his game. But it turns out he didn't have any game. Dad had an artist friend, Roy Schnackenberg, and they would golf every so often.

I tracked Roy down years later and asked him: "Was my dad a good golfer?"

His response burst my bubble. "He was terrible," Roy said. "I was worse. We were so bad, we would go out to Waveland Avenue Golf Course before the sun came up so nobody would see us golf … and so we could find our balls by tracking them in the dew on the grass. Our shots rarely made it up into the air."

Oaxaca

Roy and Chuck were great friends, sharing a passion for art, cars, and wives who liked to drink thermoses of coffee on a park bench while their boys played in the sandbox. They also shared a fear of the Cubans, based on the missiles the Russians had placed in Cuba in 1962.

Chuck and Roy had used that crisis to convince their wives that once nuclear war broke out, our families would have to move somewhere far away from the carnage and radiation. And that place would be Oaxaca in southern Mexico, right above Guatemala. Of course, they would have to drive down there and scout it out to find a suitable place for our two families to live.

On some level, Chuck probably just wanted to get out and see the world, hang out with his artist buddy, and get away from his rambunctious kids for a few days. So, they did the nearly 2,400-mile trip in our black Corvair, careening along the mountainous roads of Mexico on their way to Oaxaca. Along the way one night, they encountered several Mexican men in a black Mercedes. According to legend, the Americans in their Corvair outraced the Mexicans in their Mercedes.

After days of driving, they finally rolled into Oaxaca. Once there, they noticed something incredible: there were dozens of other pairs of American men in their late 20s and early 30s, wearing their Ray-Ban sunglasses, all looking for the same thing. Chuck and Roy thought they had the most original idea ever … and so did many other men.

The Oaxaca Factor: Never think your journey or idea is original. Chances are, there are many people just like you who are thinking and doing the same thing.

I am guilty of enjoying Chuck's absence and mildly resenting his return. I suppose I just enjoy a bit of privacy now and then—but it certainly seems indecent. I am not myself around him: I change, and this tires me after 13 years. It requires great strength to resist him and our mutual habits now. As the Boss was quoted last night, Chuck has a very Strong Personality. He is combative, spoiled, and successful. And I am tired. There are still those who only see that I'm so verbal and he's so quiet and assume from that the oddest things. I am tired, not of, but by means of, his stunts. The rage, the sulk, the exhaustion, the passivity, the dumping on me. I am to fix. Oh, buddy, fix it yourself. I can barely repair my own. And yet I am so proud of him: tough, smart, relentless, able. A great success it seems to me. He knew what he wanted to do (achievement enough), he did it (item two), and did it well (incredible).

Jamaica

Jamaica achieved its independence in 1962. At that point, investment in the Caribbean jewel increased, fancy hotels were built, and affluent Americans were invited to visit. Chuck and Ricka Dinges were among those early visitors, and they took their kids along. The James Bond classic *Thunderball* was filmed there.

The vacation was memorable because it was the first and only fancy trip we ever took as a family, and we had to pack dress clothes because dinners were lavish. We stayed at the Ocho Rios Hilton, and for the entire week at dinner we had the same tuxedoed waiter: a chubby Jamaican man named Barney. We could order whatever we wanted for dinner, even hamburgers.

I figured we were taking the trip because Dad was doing great at work and we were becoming rich, so it was time to celebrate. It was our version of Camelot. We'd spend entire days at the beach. A Jamaican guy came around and made custom straw hats for each of us. I spent so much time snorkeling in the pool that I developed a scab on my forehead and around my eyes from the swimming mask.

Mom and Dad looked happy. They looked great. Young. Cool. American. Successful. They had it all.

We drove around the island along that great road that runs along the coastline. We visited Dunn's River Falls in Ocho Rios, and I climbed to the very top holding onto a pipe that ran through the middle of the falls. I felt like King of the World when I got to the top. My parents took lots of black and white Polaroids.

We did a glass-bottom boat cruise, too, but that turned out to be terrifying. My dad was a big snorkeler—he even liked to swim in Lake Michigan back home—but unbeknown to me and Casey, he had planned to snorkel off the boat while we were watching fish eat the guts of sea urchins through the bottom of the boat. Chuck was sitting off the side of the boat when he just threw himself back into the water and disappeared. "Dad's in the water," I yelled. "He's going to drown!"

Many minutes went by and still no sign of Dad. Mom said everything would be all right; Dad was just off exploring. It was the first time I had a feeling of what it would be like to not have Dad with us, and it made me feel sick to my stomach. Dad finally reappeared as the boat tour was ending, and while it was great to see him, I was angry. How could he throw himself into the water and leave us?

That night, after we had returned to shore and were dressed up for dinner, we were walking to the dining room and passed the outdoor pool. I was to the left, and Mom was holding my hand.

Casey was to her right and holding Dad's hand. As we got to the midpoint of the pool, Casey knocked Dad off balance and he fell into the pool ... dressed up in his suit and tie.

I was shocked and thought I was about to witness the biggest spanking ever (surely it was worse than killing three pet turtles). Instead, Dad came out of the pool laughing. Mom was laughing too. My dad, still drenched in pool water, grabbed Casey around the waist and pretended to throw him in the pool. But he didn't. What the hell was going on? Nothing made any sense. But we were having fun as a family; all the tension seemed gone, and I loved that moment. I was confused yet happy.

My credentials. I am American, Midwestern, "young." I am married and have two children. My husband is a work addict, often gone when I need him, and like the rest of them, holds high executive office well in advance of his years. They call him "the kid" at the office simply because he is not fifty. We are urban, rather snotty, facile, over parental, and under attentive both simultaneously and in one blow. We are nervous, miserable, drive a Corvair, and wouldn't change places with anybody because we, like the rest of them, gave a lot of thought to it and hold with our lifestyle.

Because it is all very hard for us, we try to joke. The family drink is the martini. I shop in two places—Saks and the Sears Roebuck catalogue. We married too young. I dye my hair. That is because I am vain. Chuck has lost most of his, but he, too, is vain. Our children are entirely too healthy and we crack public jokes (borrowed from others) about how one day they'll leave us bound and gagged on the floor. We differ from others largely in one respect: we say our kids are the only two on the block who aren't geniuses.

I am 34, college trained, living in a big old apartment in Chicago. I sit in the park with my children, remembering on my good days to bring myself a thermos of coffee—coffee which I always meant to learn to drink black. I have a fair marriage and a fair hypochondriasis, at both of which I work reasonably hard. My big problem is boredom. My husband is in advertising. Sometimes I feel like we all read like stock characters in a bad novel. We go to school meetings, we always intend to do more for our political party, we never get to church. We read a lot, but the principle hobby is resting. We allege to find big parties exhausting but are offended if we are not invited. So much for that. I'm just another stiff trying to get along.

Och

My brother and I share January birthdays six days apart, and according to family lore, I came home from the hospital on his second birthday. The perfect gift, right? I'm not sure he saw it that way. Casey was a serious dude, even when he was young. He was a classic older brother. He believed in a world order, and he figured if he played by the rules and did the right thing most of the time, the world would treat him fairly and justice and happiness would prevail.

We were into different things. He hung with Dad; I preferred Mom. He loved playing sports and drawing intricate things; I liked toy cars and construction sites.

I earned the family nickname "Och" as a kid, and it came from my brother. It derived from the Vietnam War, which my brother followed more than I did in the early 1960s. "Och" (rhyming with "coach") was a reference to the Ho Chi Minh Trail, which the communist North Vietnamese had used to run weapons, ammunition, and troops through Laos and Cambodia to assist their supporters in South Vietnam. Suffice it to say, the Ho Chi Minh Trail was not a good thing. Often, I would come upon my brother fixed in concentration on a drawing or puzzle or some elaborate project. I would watch for a beat and then crawl up into his sphere. Sometimes I would make noises, and other times I would get so close he had to acknowledge my presence. Then his three-stage warning system would begin.

"You're on the Trail," he'd warn.

After a little more urging by me he'd say, "Now you're on the Minh Trail."

More agitation and he'd blurt: "You're being an OCH!"

Then a shout out to Mom saying, "Mom, Bar is being an Och. He's on the Minh Trail."

There was never a trial to determine my guilt or innocence. Mom would enter the room and say, "Ochie, knock it off. Leave your brother alone."

And I would. For about ten minutes. Sometimes Mom would tire of the Och warnings, and my brother would launch a punching war on me. That never ended well. But the pummeling felt like a win, as I had got the attention from Casey I apparently needed.

Casey is a very buttoned up kid who suffers in the manner of all nine-year-old children from an excess of Ideals. He really does think and believe that just because he does everything he's supposed to do, and does it well, that some kind of a fortunate result will therefore ensue.

*Things, of course, are not like that (I have the calluses
to prove it) and Casey feels this is Not Fair. Attempts
to counsel, advise, and pass on Wisdom: No Life is Like
That, That's the Thing about Life, Casey.*

Marbles

I developed the impressive ability to entertain myself all alone.
But that usually required a worthy target ... and that target existed
right across the alley. The Christian Science Church.

A hulking gray stone box of a building, with a huge entry
staircase and magnificent stained glass windows, the church and
its intricate windows were right across the alley from my bedroom
window. The church, designed by architect Solomon Berman, had
been dedicated in 1901 and was considered a masterpiece of Beaux-
Arts. None of that meant anything to me. I liked the geometric
design of the windows and the use of gentle pastel colors. It was
so beautiful that I wanted to break it.

I didn't much care for marbles, but combined with a slingshot
they could be fun. Even useful. One afternoon, I propped open
my window and aimed my slingshot right at the middle of the
huge glass window across the alley. I wondered if a marble could
penetrate the glass. Would a marble shatter the whole thing? I
needed to know.

I pulled my right arm back as far as I could and fired the
marble across the alley. The marble disappeared into the glass
like the sound of a bullet through glass. But the window seemed
fine. I tried another. And another. I used up all my nickel-sized
marbles ... the glass stood strong. *God*, I thought, *is impressive*.

This is a mean year for Chuck. His boss—who is so mean that he is PROUD of being known as The Butcher of Michigan Avenue—says that CHUCK is meaner than HE is. Chuck was delighted. That was the time this year HE smiled. Our kids, of course, all the while bathe in joy. They got smart, they got commitment, they got right actions, they got plans and a future. All they don't have is wide awake parents to drive them to all these places. They work on it. Casey would have the world known that he made an unassisted triple play one day last week and tied the third grade record of four goals in one day. Barnaby would show the hole where his teeth used to be. He would tell the world he hates his First Grade teacher, Mrs. Krohn.

Combat

On rare occasions, Mom and Dad went on a date night and a babysitter would come over to attempt to corral Casey and me into bed. I remember a large, middle-aged woman named Mrs. Fonseca who, when I wouldn't settle down and listen to her commands, would lay me face-down on my bed and sit on my back until I relented. She weighed a ton, and in addition to nearly breaking my back, I could barely breathe under the crush of her weight.

I complained to my parents, and they worked out a compromise with Mrs. Fonseca: she agreed to let us roughhouse until we were exhausted before she ordered us to bed. "Roughhouse" for Casey and I meant simulating an elaborate football game in the front vestibule by removing every bolster from the couches in the front living room and standing them on end to imitate NFL linemen. We would get on opposite ends of the bolsters and run plays at each other, mostly in slow motion to mimic what we saw on TV. My brother would usually serve as the announcer and color commentator, and plays generally ended up with him barreling through me into the end zone for a virtual touchdown. We would select opposing teams and players and get lost in the fantasy of our NFL re-enactment. "Gayle Sayers and the Chicago Bears cannot be stopped today," Casey would announce. "Look at the way he is cutting through the Green Bay Packers defense, like a warm knife through butter." Even though we were going nowhere near full speed, our skit would go on for hours, and by the time we were done, we were both drenched in sweat and ready to pour ourselves into bed.

My dad and I had at least one thing in common: we both loved the TV show *Combat*. A gritty 1960s war series, it featured a platoon of US soldiers fighting their way across Europe in World War II. The show was on Sunday nights, and I got to stay up a little later to watch.

It was just Dad and me because my mom would take Casey downtown to take lessons from a blind chess master named Mr. Sandman. I was happy to get Dad to myself for a few hours. I liked to lie down on the floor in the living room, fire up the big black and white TV, and watch a macho actor named Vic Morrow command his troops through violent and perilous confrontations.

The show began with a graphic of bullets spraying the screen with loud drums that made me want to get up and march in my PJs. For my dad, I'm sure it was a nice reminder of his army days in the early 1950s, and a chance to get his mind off work, his illness, and whatever else might be stressing him at the time.

My dad would prop up pillows and lean back with his legs straight out, and I would lie on my side with my head leaning on his stomach, so I was essentially watching the show sideways. But

I didn't care because I was with the coolest man in the world: my dad, Chuck Dinges. And I was spared having to go downtown with Mom and learn chess.

I was a momma's boy, except on Sunday nights when I was all about *Combat* and getting my grunt on with my dad. I was usually tucked into bed, my head still ringing from all the bombs and guns, when I heard the muffled sounds of Casey and Mom coming home from the downtown chess mission. The house never felt more peaceful and secure.

Charlie

I had a best friend growing up named Charlie Farwell. We started kindergarten at FWP together in 1963. He was a good-looking, lanky kid, whose parents dressed him up properly to go to school. While I was often dressed in a long-haul trucker's outfit, Charlie would wear a nice turtleneck shirt, matching corduroy pants, and Tretorn tennis shoes.

Charlie and I were very different, but I liked that he was scientific and could engineer anything. I had ideas; he knew how to make them happen. We were always enthusiastic co-conspirators in our plots and plans. Charlie was a quiet, kind kid. I didn't have any other friends like him.

His mom, Carol, who was friends with my mom, was super cool. She made the best hot dogs and Spaghetti O's … and sometimes she would chop up the hot dogs and put them together with the O's in one bowl! My mom was not that creative in the kitchen.

Carol would let us play in her kitchen when she was cooking, and there we invented a game called "Concoction." The object of the game was to take as many herbs and spices and oils and mix them together … and then give it a taste test. No matter what the combination, it always tasted like the worst poison imaginable. We would take one spoonful, scream in mock-death agony, run to the bathroom, lift the toilet lid, and pretend to puke our guts out.

The Farwells lived in a three-flat right across from school. Whenever Carol would tire of our noise, she sent us down to the basement of the building. It was a dank, musty place with a laundry and storage rooms for all the residents. In the back, at the end of a long hallway, was a "play room" that had a Ping-Pong table and a battery powered car that we could take turns driving. I reckoned Charlie had to be super rich because he had his own car when he was only five, and that seemed crazy.

During basement playtime, we would often get the urge to relieve ourselves, but climbing the stairs seemed burdensome, even though we were only two flights down from Charlie's apartment. We discovered, tucked in a nook off the Ping-Pong table, a dollhouse owned by a neighbor girl. It was a nice one, complete with a shingled roof, pastel painted interior, and ornate furniture inside.

We decided to test if the house was "weatherized." I stood on one side and Charlie stood on the other, and we would let loose with nature's elements. We would do that each visit down to the basement, and over time, the house started to decay. It smelled awful and started to cave in as if hit by a meteor. Kate Fisher, wherever you are today, I want to apologize for what I did to your dollhouse.

> *I am moody with Chuck and he is most cool with me. It all hurts especially now. Is this how we choose to spend those moments between disasters? So I have invited myself downtown for dinner tomorrow. A talk. Oh dear. I don't want to juggle or arrange a relationship—I just want to have one. Sometimes when I put my hand behind me, he*

*isn't there. He's up in the corner of another room looking
at me with amused surprise. I bug him since the accident*
[Casey being hit by the cab in front of the zoo]. *He
took it very hard—not as a lucky escape, as I did, but as
a slap on his grave. And so I think I understand why he
is the way he is. But I can't enjoy it. I am lonely again.
And a slightly different lonely this time. Dear Chuck.
Sometimes I am afraid he will be so remote that I will
stop loving him.*

My tendency to urinate in improper places also extended
beyond the basement. Our apartment on Wrightwood had large
cast-iron radiators that would warm our home in winter. My
bedroom had a bathroom off one end—with the hot water piped
direct from Hades—and a large walk-in closet where my parents
would store their off-season clothes. There was also a large radiator
in there. In the winter, playing in my room, I would often choose
to piss on the hot radiator rather than use the toilet, which was
just as close. There was something cool about hearing the sizzle of
the urine evaporating instantly off the hot radiator coils.

I was not a big fan of bath time, and sometimes I would
make my parents work to get me bathed. There was a large tub
in the bathroom off Mom and Dad's bedroom where they would
usually bath Casey and me, often together. One night, I decided
to make a run for it. No bath for me! I took off running in a circle
around the front of the apartment, tearing through my brother's
room, quick left into the hallway, through the vestibule, quick
left through the master bedroom, then back through the master
bathroom. I'd eluded my dad for a few laps, when I careened
around the corner into the bathroom, slipped on the floor, and
crashed face-first into the radiator by the tub.

I must have knocked myself out because when I came to, I

was sitting on top of the toilet seat, my parents were holding me up by each arm, and a doctor was putting my broken nose back into place. That was the last time I ever ran from a bath.

1966

Tried and tried to spot our house below from the air-plane, but the best I could come up with was the dome of the Elk's memorial. It made me very sad that I couldn't spot our roof. You know, I've never seen our roof. You'll have to forgive me, I'm afraid, that much of this (God maybe all) is so much self-consciousness crap, and I don't want it to be. I flee from bullshit, but it keeps popping up, spreading stomach aches in its wake. The thought of causing you pain is almost more than I can bear, because I know that when I am being me, really me, and not that horrible detached mess, that no matter what comes, happy or sad, that it's all real; and because it's real, it's bearable and worth it all. I'm finally beginning to realize how important this fight is, and God dammit I'm not going to blow it. There's something about writing with ballpoint pen on Hilton stationery that adds a note of the absurd to this whole thing, but I mean it, I mean it, and if I could pray for it, I would. I love you darling, with all my heart. I wish I could have seen our house from the air. Love, Chuck.

(A letter written by Chuck to Ricka on a business trip to New York.)

We sat down to dinner without Dad, which was not completely unusual because he often traveled to places like New York to work on advertising projects. I never knew where he was going or why, but I liked the Corgi die-cast mini sports cars he would bring me when he returned. But on this occasion, Mom announced that Dad was in the hospital and he'd be there for a few days. I blurted out: "Is Dad going to die?" Too quickly, Mom replied no, he would be fine. Casey and I shot each other concerned glances across the table.

Granny came to visit from East Lansing, Michigan, where she was a professor at Michigan State University. As a dancer in London, she had been known as Doreen Seaton, but she became Yulick when she fell in love with the dashing young attorney, Hans Leonhardt. She gave up her career and moved to Danzig to marry Hans and start a family. My mother was their masterwork.

Though she had not danced in years, Granny maintained a graceful elegance. She was always dressed up like she was going somewhere fancy—hairstyle very Jackie O, bright red lipstick, a gray turtleneck with a light cashmere sweater, a wool skirt that covered her knees, and her ballet flats. Her feet were noiseless as she moved through space.

Mom and Granny were super close, but they bickered all the time. Granny would stay in the little room off the kitchen in the back of the apartment, and I would often hear them arguing with gusto as I went to bed. It seemed Mom did most of the yelling, and I asked her one time why she was so mean to Granny. Her response? "She's difficult ... and complicated." Granny, for sure, was her daughter's mother.

But Granny was cool, too. She drove a black Corvair sedan, just like Mom and Dad. She converted her attic in her small house in East Lansing into a bedroom for Casey and me to sleep in when we visited. When she hosted us, she let us play in the big tree behind her house, and took us out for burgers at the same lunch joint every day. Then she'd drive us on the MSU campus and let us feed the ducks by the river there.

Granny visited about a week after Dad was hospitalized, and the four of us got dressed up and went downtown to Passavant Hospital. Passavant, considered the best in the city at that time, was located in the Streeterville neighborhood of the city's Gold Coast off Michigan Avenue. It was just two blocks from the Palmolive Building where Dad worked. Dad had been born at Passavant in 1931, as had Casey in 1957, and I in 1959.

I think all he cares about is his work. Chuck is angry a good deal of the time. He is basically an angry spirit, and I am basically chicken and paranoid. He has been mad without break for over a year now. And it makes me mad to have him mad all the time. Angry. I am mad as hell. What's comical is I am now as mad as he ever was. But I mean murder. I didn't even want to see the bastard: grey mean face. And when the scene gets bad enough, the sudden niceness. When it's too late and not a moment before, he wants to make you tea, play you Sinatra so you are not only angry but also guilty. Sweet innocence, the voice of all reason looks askance at The Unreasonable Lady, hollerin' away shrieking about alleged wounds.

When we saw Dad, he was in light blue-gray pajamas and a white robe. He looked considerably thinner than when we had last seen him just a week earlier. Though it was November, it was not too cold outside, so they let us walk across the street to a park where there was a quarter-mile gravel track that ran east-west, with a long bench at the east end. Mom, Dad, Granny, and Casey all sat huddled on the bench, and I looked at them. Instead of joining them, I turned and just started running.

Jim Ryun had recently run a mile in under four minutes (as a high schooler!), and I figured this would be a good chance to show Dad what I was made of. I ran effortlessly, without getting tired. Though I was dressed in long pants, a button-down shirt and my trusty saddle shoes, I felt like I could run forever. One lap. Two. Three, four … five. I'm not sure how long or far I ran that day, but I stopped only when they all got up from the bench to go back inside the hospital. I was drenched in sweat, exhilarated. The four of them didn't look quite so upbeat.

Mom went to visit Dad at the hospital the next day and brought me home a gift. Dad had taken out his fine-tip calligraphy pen and a sheet of white paper and drawn me "The Fleet of Feet Award." The award memorialized my heroic run from the prior day and featured a caricature of me looking sideways as I ran, hair flying back, and with holes in the heel of my socks from all the running.

I had made a lot of art for Mom and Dad, but this was the first time Dad had made a drawing for me. And he framed it with a simple black border. I loved it, and I knew it was more than just a drawing or an award. It was a goodbye.

A week later, Mom woke Casey and me a little earlier than normal and escorted us to the front room of the apartment. We sat on the couch with her sitting between us. She wore a robe over her sleeping clothes. She gently placed an arm around each of us and said: "I have some sad news. Your dad died last night."

The three of us just sat there in silence. No questions. No crying. Nothing.

"What about school?" Casey asked, finally.

"You're not going to school today," Mom replied.

And with that she gave Casey and me $5. She told us to get

dressed and walk down to Clark Street to get a toy at the five-and-dime store. Casey and I walked the few blocks in silence and only talked when we got to the store. We settled on Lincoln Logs, since that was something we could play with together. As we were walking back home down Wrightwood, an art teacher from school, Mrs. Meiers, drove by in her VW Bug. She stopped, rolled down the window, and asked us if we needed a ride to school. "We're not going to school today," Casey said. "Our dad died."

Mrs. Meiers' face turned white. She gave us an awkward frown and drove away. We missed several more days of school.

Funeral

I remember Mom bought Casey and me black suits and the most uncomfortable black dress shoes I'd ever worn. They made me miss my saddle shoes. As I walked down the aisle to my seat at the funeral, I felt the full-bodied discomfort of everyone's eyes on Mom, Casey, and me. Is this what life was going to be like now? Were we freaks? I didn't want sympathy. I wanted my dad back. I wanted our old life back.

The sole surviving relative in the family on either side, my father's younger sister, Jane, attended the funeral. She was a mousey, unattractive female version of my dad. She had broken her father's heart in high school by getting pregnant by a gas station attendant before dropping out of school and beginning what would be a series of failed marriages with questionable characters. Needless to say, Chuck and Jane were not close. My mother tolerated Jane and often poked fun at her in letters to friends.

The last time I saw Jane Dinges was the afternoon after my dad's funeral, when she came by our apartment on Wrightwood and grabbed a few things she said her brother wanted her to have and drove off. Casey and I never heard from her again, and that was fine.

A few days later, I returned to first grade at Francis Parker. The teacher thought it would be a nice idea if everyone brought me a small gift to welcome me back. I sat at my desk with my face in my hands and looked at all the little shiny cars and plastic soldiers my classmates had given me. After a few seconds, I swung my right arm across the desk and swept all those toys into the air and back to where they came from. I didn't need anyone's sympathy. I didn't want their eyeballs on me either. I wanted to be left alone so that I could try to get back to a normal life.

Merely Tired

By Marjorie North *(an excerpt of a novel*
Ricka was writing under a pen name)

The story of a man and woman with two young boys and how they deal with the diagnosis that her husband, Paul, has chronic leukemia.

The news hit them not neatly or cleanly with a surgical stroke, but slowly, sloppily, loopingly, in staggers and sweeps, with hopes and tears, prayers and confusion ... Paul was depressed. I have found out since that anyone with a high white count is tired, depressed, irritable. These things go together.

This was the time for bravery. I could see that. I would have to be brave for all the rest of my days, and this would be the proper time to start. But I cried. Paul was shaking too badly for any noble poses. He cried a long, long time. It was as if he were already dead. I idealized him in my mind, forgetting cross words and a million irritations. Upset as I was, I was in a way even removed—I realized I was thinking in clichés. It seemed he was "too young to die," too kind, too bright, too gifted. "Cut down in midflight." The center of the world. Even as I thought these things, the rest of me cringed with embarrassment for myself. This was all happening three months before his 30th birthday ...

If he had any time at all, he needed to work, he felt, every minute, simply to pile up money. Money ...

We have neither of us made peace with anything. Instead, we think too much. We try too hard. We talk at each across a void of subjects best left not discussed. And wonder. And we do it by ourselves, trying to be glad our friends do not guess. But then, whatever became of intuition, that facile something that makes close friends so dear?

Our insurance agent is trying wildly to sell us more coverage ... Paul takes medication which holds the blood count down well within normal range. Sometimes it only takes one pill in two months. This is how it will be. Until the day when the medicine no longer works. Then the disease will destroy his liver and his spleen and he will die ...

He has lost all patience with trivial concerns ... he has withdrawn from the rest of us, rather as if our vivid life were a little vulgar. His reactions take bizarre turns. He does of course still shake hands, but now dislikes to, and shies away from the mild kisses of friends. He feels like a leper. He feels there is something unnatural about himself. He is hounded by the fear that he may have already passed this on to our children; or that we might even have a third. To make sure that doesn't happen he simply ended that part of our life. As he does not know whether it is coming sooner or later, he does not know whether to indulge himself for the brief time remaining; or whether to build all the harder along the lines we have already laid out. A sane, conservative person, he does the latter. Will he be sorry?

Once it popped into my mind, awful as it is, that if he going to die anyway, it had better be soon, while I still have my looks, so the children and I wouldn't be alone too long. For this thought I suffered two days. Other times I gird my spirit and pray he will live forever, even if bed-ridden and helpless; and prepare myself to go out in the world and support him, as well as care for him ... I find myself drawn more closely to him, to suck out of him, as it were, every nuance that I can while he is still with me; and drawing back, trying to love him less and even hate him, so that when it comes time it will be less hard. I throw myself contentedly into my housework to try to make it as good as possible for him; and yet, at the same time, prepare myself psychologically as best I can for going back to work. One cannot do it all at once, one switches painfully from one to the other. But the pull is always there. No matter what one is thinking, it seems to be the wrong thing. There is no peace.

We have been reminded of the grim fact of individual destiny despite earthly vows. We have been reminded of all the things one knows but dislikes to remember. True, it is coming to everyone. Paul himself may be run over by a bus before the illness runs its course. But one cannot say that. The right thing is hard to come by when one of you is going to die, and the other is going to live on, and one can't decide which is worse.

Insurance we have. Strangely, while the medication is working, no doctor could tell he had leukemia. He appears in perfect health. But we are happily not being forced to play any games. We were already adequately insured before. It's a kind of grubbing everyone hates; and yet I can well imagine being forced into it ...

I think often that if he lives for, say, 20 years as a "high pressure executive," he'd never live past 40 anyway and it shall all have been a dreadful hoax, and we shall have spent our lives dealing with phantoms.

Meanwhile, I dare not fall ill. If I get nervous and bark at the children, I can see it written on Paul's face: how will she be able to cope without me when she can't cope while I'm still here? At times he wants me helpless; and at other times he wants me strong ... So we are just two ordinary people suddenly burdened by melodrama. There has been worse in life to live through, but not for us. For us, this is the worst.

One prays, but not even knowing what to pray for. I finally have arrived at a heavily qualified catch-all prayer which I mutter feverishly. I ask that he will live if he can be well and in condition to enjoy life. I ask that I be made strong as stones anyway. I ask that my children, if they must lose their father, lose him sooner before they know and love him too well to ever love another; and, at the same time, they lose him later, when he has had more time to mold them to be like himself. I pray I don't get peculiar.

And where is the neurasthenia, the dulling of feeling, that the doctors promised would come? The burden of pain is enormous, and it has been with us every day now for more than half a year. They promised me it would recede, that the mind builds walls against that which it cannot bear. Why couldn't that have been so?

We try to know each other, try to help each other, and really can't, except in the preservation of those manners which are reassuring by their very existence through all calamity. Strength and wisdom are the goals, and beyond that everyone is really as alone as I am …

Life after Dad

I was seven and Casey was nine as we tried to establish a new way of living with Mom. I learned how to make her tea and toast, and I would bring it to her in bed in the mornings as she was waking up. Casey and I made a concerted effort to fight less, but that was always a game-time decision.

One day, Mom told us the story of what led up to Dad's death. In 1961, when we were very young, Dad was diagnosed with leukemia and was told he had one to five years to live. We were lucky when he lived the full five. This also explained the motorcycle, the crazy trip down to Mexico, the lavish trip to Jamaica, the long nights my dad spent downtown fulfilling his ambition.

Chuck had succeeded. At age 33, he was a creative director at a hot, growing ad agency in the go-go '60s. He signed up for the maximum life insurance, so Mom received $100,000 when he died. That was some serious money in 1966, but mom was worried about finances. She was worried about everything.

She got a job working as a researcher in the same place Dad had worked, the Palmolive Building downtown. The building's name was changed to The Playboy Building, and that was Mom's new employer. She brought home stationery and envelopes from Playboy, and I would write her letters telling her how much I missed her, how much I needed her. And she would write back "letters to Bar-Bar." Only she got to call me that.

I would get home from school before she returned from work, and I would wait for her on the church stairs next to our home. I would look to the east, like a dog waiting for its owner to return from an errand, watching all the working people get off the bus a block away on Stockton Drive, the main north-south road through Lincoln Park. When I saw her, I'd jump up from the church stoop and ran down Wrightwood to greet her. I would hold her hand for the short walk home. I enjoyed this new wrinkle in life.

But it got harder for Mom. A few months after Dad passed, her Mom died, and that left her all alone. No family left to reach out to. As much as Granny and Mom argued all the time, she was Mom's life coach and the one who knew her best.

Mom grew dark and sad. She hardly wrote at all. She looked thin, less glamorous. She kept up with the coffee, cigarettes, and red wine.

1967

ONE RAINY WEEKEND DAY, about a year after Dad died, Mom took Casey and me a few blocks down Clark Street to see a movie in color—a racecar flick called *Grand Prix*, starring James Garner. The movie had great racing scenes and lots of crashes, and a side story about Garner having an affair with an ex-teammate's wife. Casey and I came out of that movie revving with energy, and we skipped down Wrightwood splashing through puddles. Well behind us, Mom walked slowly, hands in the front pockets of her coat, sunglasses hiding her eyes, looking grim.

"What's wrong, Mom?" I asked her.

"We'll talk when we get home."

As we entered the vestibule, Mom sat down on the floor, still wearing her wet coat. Casey and I were silent, looking at her, listening.

"I can't do this alone," she said. "I need more help from you two. This isn't working. I need you to need less and do more. I need to be able to take care of myself."

We sat there in silence for a long time, on the floor, still in our wet coats. Mom was suffering, and that was hard to see. She seemed to be saying we made it worse, and that was hard to hear because I knew we woke up each day and tried to help her. That was the first sign that in the House of Dinges, The Queen was not well.

A few months later, Chicago got hit with one of its biggest snow storms ever, nearly two feet of snow in one night. There were mountains of snow everywhere, and the city was buried.

Cars weren't moving anywhere. And we were short on food. Mom told Casey and me she needed us to put on our snow clothes, get the sled out of the basement, and get to the Shop & Save grocery store two blocks to the north on Diversey Avenue. We had never shopped at the grocery store before, but Mom gave us a list of things and $20 and sent us off down the alley. We crawled those two blocks on our stomachs, inching along like soldiers in battle.

We were exhausted by the time we made it to the Shop & Save, and we must have asked for help finding things because most of the items on Mom's list we had never heard of. Orange marmalade?

Hours later we returned home with the goods. Mom toasted our heroism with hot chocolate. I had a warm feeling, maybe things were turning around. We could help her. We would be okay.

1968

I MADE A CONCERTED EFFORT to help Mom after her vestibule meltdown. Casey and I did everything we could think of to team up to make her life easier. But our life together felt different now as we were no longer a foursome and, therefore, unable to break up into pairs; it was three of us all the time.

One annual ritual was our trip to the doctor for our school physicals. Mom drove us to downtown Chicago to see Dr. Robert Mendelson, the middle-aged man who gave me and Casey our inspections. The trip was tense because Mom was not the best driver, especially with a nine-year-old and an eleven-year-old in the back seat, sans seatbelts, giving each other the business the whole way.

Visits to the doctor didn't make much sense at that age, since there was so little to examine. A tad more height and weight—noted—but then the doctor would want to feel around to make sure everything was in the right place ... but there was very little happening on that front either. To save time, the doctor examined us one after the other in the same room.

The appointment ended with Casey and me being asked to piss in separate buckets. This took a while, since Mom and the doctor were standing there in the sterile office and I wasn't used to pissing under such pressured circumstances. Finally the job was done, and as my mom was saying her farewells to the doctor, I reached over and poured my piss into Casey's bucket.

Mom saw this and yelled, "Barnaby, what are you DOING? What's the matter with you?"

I was stunned by her anger because I felt I had done one of the smartest things ever: combine the piss and save time. One test. We eat the same stuff. We're brothers! If there's a problem, we'd return to see the doctor together.

We drove home in silence, my mom staring straight ahead behind her black Ray-Ban glasses, and Casey shaking his head next to me, enjoying my apparent stupidity. Ochie had outdone himself. A part of me still felt kind of proud. I was an out-of-the-bucket thinker. My brain didn't work like everyone else's, and that was a good thing.

Then There Were Two

I have no memory of being told that Mom died, or attending her funeral. I remember only that Mom went into the hospital for surgery to repair an ulcer. She worried a lot, didn't eat right, smoked cigarettes, and drank too much coffee and wine. In her journal, she referred to this as "The Radiator Disease."

> *I am the most unsuccessful product yet of Nazi Germany.*
> *I take Lomotil, Libriums, aspirins, Mylicons, No-Doz*
> *… Radiator Disease good, nerves hanging in tatters.*
> *When I dope myself sufficiently that my bowels can resist*
> *my lifestyle, it is apparently my thyroid balance that is*
> *affected. I am flying around, out of breath, accomplish-*
> *ing and accomplishing, with no appetite, no sleep, no*
> *rest, no peace. Pant pant.*

Mom died on February 21, 1968, the day after her 37th birthday. The cause of death "cardiac asystole" during a surgical procedure for "ruptured abdominal abscess, generalized peritonitis." She essentially had a heart attack during a routine surgery to fix an ulcer. A 37-year-old woman properly cared for would normally not die from such a procedure. But these were not normal times.

During Mom's brief hospitalization, so short that we never once visited, there was a parade of young women who came to the apartment to look in on us and make sure we had something to eat. They were my mom's coworkers from Playboy. Stylish and pretty women, like her, but a few years younger. They all had long straight blonde or dark brown hair, and they wore those Laura Petri slacks that fit tightly on the legs, ending a few inches above their ankles. I convinced myself they were all Playboy bunnies, and they were in the apartment to distract us, to keep our mind off Mom. They remained for a few weeks after Mom died.

One morning, I was playing in my room when I heard the thud of a hard object against the wall, a sound that reminded me of good times at the construction sites. It was the sound of demolition. Wham. A brief pause. Wham. The sound of rubble falling to the ground. I stepped across the thin hallway and there was Casey, hockey stick in hand, using it to create a big hole in the wall of his room. At this point, he'd removed a few square feet of plaster and was getting down to the slats.

"What are you doing?" I asked.

"I'm taking my anger out on the wall. Wanna help?" he offered.

I shook my head and went back into my room. I wasn't angry. And I wasn't yet sad. I was still in shock. I didn't know what might happen next.

A few more days passed and Casey convinced me to commit my first official crime—theft. Casey was a serious collector of baseball cards, so when Topps came out with a cool new set of cards with a jazzy design, Casey decided he wanted the entire set

NOW. But he needed $20. He came into my room one evening with a one dollar bill and told me that it was the same as a $20 bill, just in a different design. He'd already checked the purse of the nice young lady who was looking after us that night, and he suggested he'd distract her in the kitchen at the back of the apartment, and I could swap a one dollar bill for a $20 from her purse in the vestibule.

I did the deed, my brother was happy, and the Playboy lady didn't seem to notice. But going to sleep that night I knew I'd done a shitty thing. Humor was my calling card, not crime. I drifted off to sleep that night thinking about an unhappy life of crime and hoping I might avoid that fate.

part two

Unbeknownst to Casey and me, a committee had formed at Francis W. Parker School to determine what to do with the orphaned Dinges boys. The priority was to try to keep us at school, since that would provide some continuity. We were both doing well there and had friends. The committee was horrified by the thought of us ending up in the suburbs. Skokie? Hell no! It was Parker or bust for us.

My mom had updated her will, but it had us going to live with Roy and Barb Schnakenberg, her good friends who lived two blocks away ... but Roy and Barb were in the process of getting divorced. There were no surviving relatives, so a family would have to step up and take us.

In taking us, the family would not have to worry about paying for school; Mom had left more than $100,000 in her accounts. This money would pay for school, incidental costs, and the guardians could petition our trust officer for approval to access the rest of the money. Also, my brother and I would receive a Social Security check each month that the family could deposit in their accounts, a benefit the government provided to us as orphans, since our parents would not be accessing Social Security benefits later on. These monthly checks would keep coming until we turned 21, as long as we remained full-time students.

After many days the "Keep the Dinges Boys at Francis Parker" campaign found a taker: the Majewskis, a Jewish family living two blocks away who also had three boys at Parker. They lived in an old two-and-a-half story Brownstone on a small street called Roslyn Place between Lincoln Park and Clark Street, less than a half mile from Lake Michigan.

The Majewskis

I arrived at the Majewski home with the clothes on my small fourth-grade frame, and something I tucked under my baggy sweatshirt—my trusty Big Ben alarm clock. This was my prized possession at the time because I knew that when the alarm went off early the next morning, I would get up and go to school. And if I did that, I would be okay.

Alan Majewski was a world-renowned harpist and, at that time, the lead harpist for the respected Chicago Symphony Orchestra. His wife, Darlene, dabbled in black-and-white photography in her basement darkroom. Their sons, Doug, Mark, and Ron, were 15, 13, and 10, respectively. Casey was 11 and I was nine.

Alan was a kind, sweet man. He had a full head of jet-black hair and a sharp nose and jaw that gave him a striking, handsome appearance. The greatest harpist in the world, his life revolved around his instrument. Darlene ran the house and Alan lost himself in his music.

Darlene was a big-boned, masculine looking woman with thinning hair that she would bolster with a "fall," a fake swathe of hair that would hang off the back of her head. She dressed herself up with bright red lipstick, and her head would wobble slightly when she sat still. She liked to drink Scotch routinely and play poker with local men at various games in the neighborhood. She liked card games, Yahtzee, and watching TV in her upstairs bedroom. She never cleaned house, and she cooked for volume not flavor. She allowed dirty laundry to pile up at the bottom of the laundry chute that ran from the third floor to the basement, only doing the laundry when the pile got so high that the chute got clogged. When she did laundry, she did it all together (no separating the whites from the colors), so clothes took on a common gray-blue hue over time.

Our welcome to the Majewskis was not a warm and fuzzy one. We were not afforded the sympathy or kindness one might think we were due having just lost our parents. Darlene informed us that their taking us in was both a gallant act and a tremendous burden. We would need to work every day for the privilege of living there. Our daily chores would include cleaning the dishes and kitchen after each dinner and walking their two large dogs. Weekend chores would include cleaning the rest of the house, including the four bathrooms, and sometimes the basement where there was a partial dirt floor. The Majewski boys would be spared these chores, except occasional dish washing duty.

"That's not fair," Casey said to Darlene upon learning about our new responsibilities.

"Tough," Darlene responded. "Life isn't fair. You of all people should understand that."

"I hate it here," Casey said. "I don't want to live here."

"Well that's too bad," Darlene shot back. "No one else wanted you. You are an ungrateful little shit."

I watched this exchange in silence. While I agreed with everything Casey said, I thought the best approach was to go along and see how it unfolded. Maybe we could work our way into the Majewskis' better graces and it might get better. It was 1968, remember, and Casey was cut more from the Bobby Seale school of rebellion, and I was more from the Abby Hoffman school of humor.

The Majewski house was one of those 100-foot deep, 25-foot wide stone buildings in Chicago that were dark inside. It connected directly to another home to the east, so there were no windows on that side, while on the other side, the windows were denied light by a four-foot-wide gangway between the home and the one to the west.

The entry to the house was a small vestibule cluttered with hanging coats, with a living room to the right, and a middle room where Alan played the harp. There was a small bathroom to the left, and a large kitchen in the back. A large staircase to the left led to the second floor (there was also an emergency staircase off the back of house), where there was a bedroom in back, a sitting room, a small bathroom, and then a hallway leading to another small bathroom and bedroom, and then a small master bedroom. There was a stairway to the third floor, which was only half a floor, with a small bedroom and bathroom. The walls of the house lacked the colorful art and large oil paintings I'd known at my parents' Wrightwood apartment.

Casey and I were put together on the third floor, where our tiny bedroom had barely enough room for two twin beds side by side, and two small desks jammed against the wall by a window off the gangway. As isolated as I felt up there, it was comforting to go to sleep next to Casey and share thoughts about the day we had and the situation we were in.

Casey's prized possession was Dad's Zenith Royal 3000 Trans-Oceanic Radio, through which we listened to programs from all over the world when we went to bed. Most of the time we couldn't understand a word we were hearing, but we liked the thought of listening to what Dad had heard, and imagine a dying man trying to reach out to the world and absorb as much as he could before his departure.

The Majewski dogs were huge. They were a mother and son team, Tango and Billy respectively. Tango, an Alaskan Malamute, was so overfed that her stomach nearly dragged on the ground when she walked. Billy looked like a Sheepdog but was a Malapoo, the product of a Standard Poodle in the neighborhood that had come together with Tango. That couldn't have been pretty.

Tango had the disturbing habit of letting anyone come into the house but chasing them and trying to bite them when they left. Luckily, since she was so fat from lying around all day, she was easy to outrun. On the other hand, Billy packed the force of an entire dogsled team. Both dogs were so big and strong that they needed to be walked separately, and I would have to wrap the leather leash around my torso to keep the dogs under control for the brief walk down Roslyn Place east to Lincoln Park.

The weekday routine was to wake up early, thanks to my trusty Big Ben, and dress quickly in whatever I could find that was least dirty. My clothes were hand-me-downs that had been through many wears and the gray-laundry treatment, so I would leave the house feeling dressed in prison wear. I'd grab a quick bowl of cereal in the kitchen and head out the front door for the four-block walk down Clark Street to school.

I'd often run to school because I couldn't wait to get there, even though fourth grade was no picnic. Mrs. Helen Martin was a tall, imperious woman who taught us Greek history. She reminded me of my Granny, so I tried to behave and do well in her class. Like most kids, I liked recess the best because we were let outside where there was a playground filled with dangerous Jungle Gyms and a field big enough for a touch football game. I loved the football games because I was faster than almost all the other kids. Being short and slight meant they could barely catch me, let alone touch me. I felt powerful out on the playground and always hated it when the bell rang and the teachers called us inside.

I loved lunchtime because my estate paid for a pass that allowed me to eat anything I wanted … and the food was much better than whatever I would encounter at the Majewski dinner table that night.

If there was an after-school activity, I would try it. They had something called Midget Soccer for kids between third and seventh grade, and I signed up for that. We had patriotic uniforms with blue and white stripes, and a V-neck that was red. I loved soccer because maneuverability and ball control were easy for me, since I was so close to the ground. I always felt I could have an impact on the game.

By the time I was living with the Majewskis, the construction sites were fewer, and they had started to put fences around them. Even if any open sites had remained, I was unable to play. I had to get home to do chores, including walking the dogs, as well as do my homework up in my room until someone hollered that dinner was ready.

Dinners at the Majewski house were an uneasy free-for-all. Food would be cooked in large vats in the back of the kitchen. There was a long wood table in the kitchen with enough room for eight. Sloppy Joes were a staple, which sounds good, but when the meat mush and soft buns were dropped in the middle of the table, it was like eating amid a pack of hungry dogs, and I was the runt. The Majewski boys would often take multiple sandwiches before Casey and I could get in for one.

There was very little conversation, and all I heard were the disgusting sounds of lips smacking and food being chewed way too loud and fast. The Majewski kids would finish eating quickly and disappear from the table, often to go upstairs to watch TV in their parents' room. Casey and I would be left to clean the kitchen, and although the meal was incredibly simple, the mess seemed to be enormous. Dishes piled up in the sink, including pots that were impossible to get clean. Food debris was spread everywhere. It could easily take 30 minutes to clean the dishes, wipe down the counters, and vacuum the kitchen carpet. Darlene would inspect our cleaning effort, and we could go back upstairs to our room if she approved. I couldn't wait to get back to my schoolwork.

Only a few months after Casey and I went to live at the Majewski house, the Democratic Convention came to Chicago. I didn't know much about politics beyond that my mother cried the day JFK was killed, and she later supported LBJ. The whole city seemed up for grabs with long-haired hippy dudes and halter top-wearing chicks walking up and down Clark Street and camping out in Lincoln Park.

Though we were nearly five miles from the heart of downtown where all the protesting was happening, Darlene told us to stay out of the park. Well, that was an invitation to go to the park, especially with Tango or Billy in tow. For that brief period for a few days in August, I would take the dogs for the longest walks to see the mellow haze of smoke billowing over the lagoon in the park and the young campers cavorting in their tents or rolling around on the grass. The protesters seemed totally benign; I couldn't see what all the fuss was about.

1969

DARLENE AND ALAN DETERMINED THAT with the addition of Casey and me, they didn't have a big enough house or car. They convinced the trustee of our estate they needed to tap our resources to get a bigger car, finish off the third floor of their house, and add a large bedroom upstairs. While they were at it, they would add a rooftop garden and put light-brown wood paneling over all the plaster walls.

For a car, they bought a black Checker Marathon with red interior. The Marathon was the cab being driven around Chicago back then, and it had little seats that could pop up in the middle to accommodate additional riders. The Majewskis had their Marathon custom-made with a bench in the middle so it could seat nine people. For added flexibility, the bench was designed to be folded forward so that Alan could fit his harp into the back if he angled the instrument just right. Over the years, Alan suffered six hernias loading and unloading that massive harp, even though he usually got help from one or more of us.

The house addition was a six-month project that would go on for years. Darlene hired a rag-tag group of workers who reminded me of the hippies I'd seen sleeping out in the park. They liked to drink, and when they knocked off early (after starting midmorning), Darlene would drink with them.

The only good thing about the project was the kitchen was generally out of commission, so Alan would peel off singles and send us off to Clark Street to eat burgers, hot dogs, and French fries for dinner. The Majewski kids would get $2 each, and Casey and I would each get $1. When Casey challenged the unfairness of the nightly food allowance, he was told the Majewski kids got more because they were bigger, which was true. Majewskis were larger mammals than Dingeses.

Whereas the Majewski kids favored McDonald's, I preferred Zyggy's Hot Dogs because it had a jukebox and a girl working there who had gorgeous breasts that would jiggle when she leaned over to prepare the hot dog and fries. She and her boyfriend ran the place, and they were always playing great music and arguing in a friendly way behind the counter. My favorite song was Norman Greenbaum's "Spirit in the Sky," which I would request every visit. The song was gospel rock, but I just liked it because it sounded cool. I didn't even know who Jesus was.

With the construction project came another job for me ... to ensure a white tarpaulin covered the stairs up to the second floor so that the carpet wouldn't be ruined by all the dirt and debris. Four or five times a day, I would climb the stairs one by one and make the sure tarp was tucked in tight.

One day, after a lot of traffic on the stairs, things got a little loose, and Tango, who struggled up and down stairs due to her tremendous weight, lost her footing on the way down, rolled over several times, and ended up in a heap on the landing. Tango moaned in pain as Darlene grabbed me by the wrist and dragged me upstairs to her bedroom. Using a shoe with a flat heel, she pulled me over her lap as she sat on the bed and beat my rump until it was raw. "Don't you ever do that to Tango again!" she yelled. "Now get upstairs and go to bed."

The sun was still up as I got under the covers, crying from the beating and my general unhappiness. I heard Doug, the eldest Majewski boy, who was 16 at the time, complaining to Darlene about the beating. She ordered him out of her room and told him to mind his own business. I went to sleep wet from tears and a bloody and blistered behind.

Darkroom Doug

Doug was a scientific kid who liked to take apart car engines and play around in Darlene's basement darkroom. I hated it down there, with its musty air and chemical smells wafting out from the darkroom, but Doug stayed in there for hours, and he took Casey with him to teach him how to develop black and white photographs. This was handy because Casey spent most of that summer grounded for allegedly lying to Darlene.

In addition to the grounding, Casey's punishment was that he had to go to sleep every night at 6:30 pm, which was almost impossible to do in the Chicago summer when it's hot as hell and the sun doesn't set until 9:00 pm or later. There was no air conditioning in the house, and Casey would swelter in the bedroom on the third floor, stripping down to nothing and laying in bed with just a sheet over him. I would often go upstairs and sit on the side of his bed as he lay there, listening to his furious commentary.

I was struck that he spent much of that summer down in the darkroom during daylight, and then in his bed as the sun burned in the evening sky. I appreciated Doug doing what he could to help Casey, because I felt helpless to do so.

Miami with the Majewskis

Perhaps it was a family bonding exercise, or maybe just a move to get away from the home reconstruction project, but the Majewskis decided we should pack up the spanking-new Marathon and drive from Chicago to Miami to visit relatives. Alan drove with Darlene at his side in the front seat. Casey and I were in the middle on the folding bench, and the three Majewski kids sat in the back. Darlene had two things she liked to do on a long car ride: try to identify the license plates of cars from all 50 states and kiss her husband each time the odometer added another 100 miles. These habits would prove annoying over the 1,400-mile drive that took two straight days.

The trip was going fine until the youngest Majewski, Ron, kept falling asleep in the back and leaning on one of his older brothers to his left or right. They didn't like that, so headlocks and fistfights kept erupting in the back. Ron was moved up to the middle bench where he kept napping and leaning, which meant he was crushing me. I realized that if I lay crosswise along the floor of the Marathon, I could contort myself into a comfortable position and maybe get some sleep myself. The floor was a challenge too, as I felt the rumble of road and had to contend with the eight gnarly feet of four older "brothers," as well as wrappers and other debris. But there was something wonderful about the rhythm of the highway and my desire to escape the situation that lulled me off into an extended sleep.

When I awoke, we were stopping for dinner at a place called Kentucky Fried Chicken. *Yet we were in Alabama.* The Majewskis got two big buckets of chicken, which the kids attacked like animals as we sat around a large picnic table around the back of the restaurant. It was a warm evening. I looked over at the table next to us and saw a large family gathered around an immense pyramid of mashed potatoes. That family was eating off the mound of spuds with dull, bored expressions.

I made eye contact with the young girl in the family; she was younger than my ten years. She had stringy, dirty-blond hair and noticeable gaps between her teeth. She stepped over to me and asked for a piece of chicken. I felt frozen. We had plenty of chicken, but I felt afraid of this little girl and ashamed that she was hungry and I was not. I started crying and waved her back to her table.

Darlene noticed and asked, "What's your problem? Why are you crying?"

"That girl was begging for food. I didn't know what to do."

"Well, you don't cry like a little baby. You need to grow up."

Soon after we got back in the Marathon for the drive through Florida. I tucked myself in on the floor and wrapped my arms tightly around my chest to give myself a hug.

When we finally arrived at Miami Beach for what had been advertised as a family vacation, I found out I was really at music camp. We were staying at Alan's mother and sister's house—a two-story square house near Flamingo Park. Alan's mom played the harp, as did his nephew, David, who was Casey's age, as well as his niece, Sophie, who was my age and looked like a young, tanned Raquel Welch.

Darlene and Alan dropped us off and drove away in the Marathon, and our month of "music" began. The Majewski kids all played instruments: Doug played the harp, Mark played the piano, and Ron played the violin. Casey and I were completely non-musical, and the Majewski parents often reminded us of that failing in our early upbringing.

We were also not Jewish, or at least not Jewish enough (Hans' battles with Nazis apparently got us no points). I never remember the word "religion" used in the Dinges home, and the only time I went to church was when my parents died. The Majewski kids all studied the Torah and got Bar Mitzvahed. We were never given the opportunity, and that added to our feeling as outcasts.

Each morning in Miami began with a breakfast of oranges and bananas, and then at least two hours practicing our instrument before we were allowed to step outside. Alan's mom, Nettie, was a short, powerful woman who had reared the world's greatest harpist. Having to teach me piano was, I'm sure, a low in her musical life. She would show me a few notes on the piano then get up and walk off into the kitchen muttering. In a month, I learned to play one song on the piano ... "Mary Had a Little Lamb."

By 11 or so in the morning, we would be released and all the boys except me went out and did something fun, like go fishing in David's Boston Whaler. I was not allowed to go because I couldn't swim, was too young, too small, and there wasn't enough room. So, I was stuck at the house with Alan's mother and his sister, Denise, and the lovely Sophie. Sophie had that perpetual Florida tan, and the body of a young gymnast. We would listen to 45s (although Nettie would tell us to "turn off the coon music" whenever we played the Jackson Five) and take walks around the neighborhood.

I liked Sophie so much that I wanted to show off for her. One day as we were walking, I came upon a big gray swirl of a structure hanging in a bush off the sidewalk. "Watch this!" I said, as I walked up to the hole in the football-sized attraction. I gave it a mighty whack and out came a hornet the size of a small bird. It stung me on my side, and I felt my entire skin erupt in pain. I rolled on the sidewalk crying until Sophie got me up, and I walked home.

After I had spent many days with the women, David said he'd hang out for a few afternoons with me. He said he'd teach me how to play stickball—a version of baseball involving broomsticks as bats and a tennis ball. They would play at the handball courts out in the park. But David said we needed to get me a stick first, so we got on bikes and rolled down the alleys nearby in search of a broom or mop. David stopped halfway down one alley and pointed to a nice thick mop hanging off a second floor porch.

"Go get it," he told me.

I could hear women speaking Spanish as I climbed the rickety wood stairs. I reached for the broom and could see an older lady looking at me through a screen door. She screamed at me, but I grabbed the broom and shot down the stairs. I tossed it to David and hopped on my bike, which was Sophie's Schwinn, and started peddling madly. I looked back and saw the old lady was closing fast. David got between me and her, slowing her down with a few menacing waves of the mop. A few minutes later, we were in the park, cutting off the mop head and learning how to play fastpitch.

"You're a fast little fucker," David told me later. "I might be able to use you again."

One evening near sunset, David asked Nettie and Denise if he could take me for a little bike ride. They didn't care, so David and I set out with nothing but a burlap bag over his shoulder.

"What are we doing?" I asked.

"Creating a big surprise," he said.

We biked a few blocks over to a burger joint called King Castle (not to be confused with White Castle). This place served ordinary food to the masses, and that included all the stray cats that hung out at the back of the joint foraging for food around the garbage bins. There were about 15 cats of all sizes and colors feeding around the base of the garbage cans.

"Go get one," David said, tossing me the burlap bag.

"For what?" I asked.

"You'll see."

That burlap bag was about big enough to hold me inside, so I rolled it halfway up and stretched it across my chest before I tore into the pack of cats. Most of them scattered, but a mid-sized one seemed particularly intent on finishing its meal, and that's the one I sacked.

As I rolled on the ground trying to control the wild cat, David appeared and tied off the bag and threw it over his shoulder.

"Follow me," he said.

We walked a block to a row of newspaper dispensers. David dropped a nickel into the Miami Herald box and opened its metal door. He shook the cat out of the bag and into the box, then shut the door on the newspaper dispenser. The cat was shaking the entire newspaper hut from the inside and unleashing loud screeches as we walked back to our bikes.

"That," David said, "is going to surprise the hell out of the newspaper delivery man in the morning."

I could hardly sleep that night as I thought of the sunrise surprise, the delivery man screaming when the cat jumped out of the box, and the cat running to freedom and another square meal at the King Castle.

I felt like I was the king. For a day, anyway.

Baseball Rules

In 1969, Chicago started to recover from the embarrassment of the riots and police beatings surrounding the Democratic National Convention, and the Chicago Cubs made a serious run at getting to the World Series. They had a team full of future Hall of Famers, but there wore down and choked in August. Ultimately, the New York Mets broke their hearts and won their own World Series. As with all things in life, things can be going great, but they can suddenly fall apart for no apparent reason.

Baseball became my new favorite sport, eclipsing soccer, and I would sneak upstairs some afternoons to the second floor to watch Cubs games on a big black and white TV at the back of the house. It was a lesser traveled part of the house, so I was usually safe and alone there for a while.

Also big then was a baseball board game called Strat-O-Matic that allowed you to manage your own Major League team and game using dice and player cards. The player cards were based on statistics and player performance, and the dice determined what happened when a pitcher and batter squared off. The game was incredibly realistic, and it could take an hour to complete a full nine-inning game. You could also play and score the game by yourself, which was good for me since the older kids usually didn't want me outmaneuvering them with my managing skills.

Alan came into the kitchen one Saturday morning and dropped the latest version of Strat-O-Matic on the table, including the entire set of teams from the prior year. The Majewski kids picked their teams, and I selected the New York Mets, in part because they had my favorite non-Cubs player, pitcher Tom Seaver. I loved Seaver's smooth and efficient pitching motion. With a nickname like Tommy Terrific, what was not to like? The Mets that year also had an outfielder named Cleon Jones who hit .340—by far the best in the league—and his Strat card was the best I'd ever seen.

Mark, the middle Majewski kid, proposed I make a trade for Cleon Jones. He was offering two Baltimore Orioles outfielders, Ron Blair and Don Buford, who each batted around .290 that year. Mark insisted the two Orioles outfielders were more valuable than my one Mets outfielder. But this was Cleon Jones! I liked his card so much that all I had to do was stare at it; I didn't even have to play it to enjoy it.

I told Mark I would think about it. That evening I got called to meet Darlene in her room for a conversation. This was unusual, since nearly all of my dealings with her were in the kitchen. I entered to find her sitting in the middle of her bed, watching a large color TV to her right.

"I understand Mark offered to trade two of his cards for one of yours and you refused," she said.

"I didn't say no," I responded. "I'm just not sure I want to do it."

"What's the matter with you?" Darlene wondered. "We take you in, give you a nice place to live, make you a part of our family, and yet you are so selfish."

"I'm not selfish," I responded.

"Is that all you have to say?" she asked.

"I don't want to trade Cleon Jones. Not for two average players," I said.

There was a long pause as she sat there staring at me from her bed, her head wobbling sideways like a bobble-head doll.

"You don't own the baseball cards. I do. So, you are going to give Mark the Cleon Jones card and that's final."

I ran upstairs to my room and contemplated tearing up the Cleon Jones card. Instead, I went to the top of the stairs and threw the card down from the third floor. "Mark, you can have it!" I yelled and went back into my room to mourn. And that was the end of my promising career as a Strat-O-Matic manager.

Alan Assists

I had almost no one-on-one time with Alan Majewski. His life consisted of practicing the harp at home (where he also gave lessons), rehearsing with the Chicago Symphony Orchestra, performing at concerts, consulting at Lyon & Healey (a musical instrument company headquartered in Chicago), making recordings for commercials, and running errands for Darlene in the neighborhood.

His favorite thing seemed to be walking to the neighborhood Ace Hardware store, where he was on first-name terms with the entire staff. Sometimes Alan would ask me if I wanted to join him on the hardware run, and I always said yes.

Alan liked to tinker with things around the house. He loved to bring home some new appliance that the hardware store just got in, like an Amana Radarange Microwave Oven. That was perfect because Darlene could heat up questionable leftovers in less than three minutes! I was amused that the Amana oven came with its own radiation detector wand that could be used to sweep around the door of the oven to measure excess release of radiation. What a great addition to the kitchen! I made a point of keeping a distance from that contraption.

There were times when Alan showed me special kindness. Somehow, I had never learned how to ride a bike. Perhaps my parents figured I got into enough trouble in the neighborhood on foot and wheels would only extend the range of my terror. When Alan learned this, he took me out to Lincoln Park on an oversized Schwinn bike, put me on the seat and shoved me off down the sidewalk, where fear of falling kept me upright long enough to determine that I could now ride a bike at age 11.

Alan also shared with the me the kindness of teaching me how to properly wipe my ass after crapping. One day, without prompting, he showed me that if you fold a few sheets of toilet paper and spit in the middle, you can achieve a softer, cleaner result.

Then there was the night when Darlene was out in the neighborhood playing poker, and I was downstairs in the front room in my pajamas enjoying a rare non-stressful moment in the house.

As I enjoyed the tranquility, free of Darlene, a sadness crept over me: I missed my parents. I felt their absence in my chest, and I started to cry, alone on the couch.

Alan walked by and, seeing me weeping, asked what was wrong. I thought about not telling him, thinking it may hurt his feelings.

"Bar, what's wrong? You can tell me," Alan said softly.

"I'm sad because I miss my mom and dad," I said.

Alan walked over, sat next to me, and hugged me. I hugged him back, and then he pulled me onto his lap and rocked me gently.

"It's okay, Bar," Alan said. "I know you miss them. You should feel sad. I understand."

Alan held me for a long time, and it was memorable because it was the one and only time I felt loved in that house.

1970

I WAS EXCITED WHEN THE summer ended and the school year began. That was especially true living in the Majewski house. Many of my classmates I'd known since kindergarten in 1963. We came up together. I even had girls who were my friends, but mostly my fun was trying to make the guys laugh. True, my parents were no longer around for The Barnaby Show, but that didn't mean I was going out of business. I was looking for new material, audiences, and ways to win.

In third grade, I had led a rebellion against our teacher—a stocky little man named Larry Jacobson. Mr. Jacobson would start the day by going to the blackboard and writing BOYS and GIRLS in block letters at opposite ends of the board. Each time anyone of that gender acted up, he scratched a line on the board, and whichever gender generated five scratches by recess would have to stay inside. Each day, the boys would have a bunch of digits on the boards and the girls would have none, so we would miss recess. (I had complained to my mom about the unfairness, but she ignored me, especially since I was earning some of the strokes.) After Dad died, Mom let Casey and me start to grow a little hair, kind of bowl cuts with bangs, Beatles style, and Mom would cut our hair every few weeks. One day, Mr. Jacobson made fun of my haircut in front of the whole class. "Did you cut your hair in your sleep?" he asked me. Mom didn't like that very much, so she came to school to tell the teacher directly and put him on notice that she was aware of the mistreatment of the boys in the class.

But the boys recess ban continued. The worst part was that we could look out at the playground from the second-story window and see Mr. Jacobson sitting on the bench watching the girls, often with a few of them sitting on his lap. I needed to free the boys and save the girls, so one day I noticed that the smartly designed school had exterior window ledges that were almost two feet deep. I cranked open the classroom windows and coaxed as many boys as possible out onto the ledge to yell niceties at Mr. Jacobson. We got his attention, and when he saw virtually all the third grade boys out on the window ledges calling him out, he yelled for us to get back inside. But other teachers were out for recess and they noticed the rebellion.

A short time later, I was in Principal Scott Segner's office. I was in trouble for The Window Rebellion, but I was granted an audience to go in detail about all the crazy stuff happening in our classroom. I was suspended for a few days (just fine by me), and Jacobson was forced to end the boy ban at recess. Win!

Years later, I was not surprised to learn that Larry Jacobson died in a Florida prison while serving a life sentence for adopting a young girl and using her as his sex slave.

Rebel without Cause

My reputation as a disrupter followed me into fourth grade, but I was granted some license because school officials figured I was blowing off steam after the death of my dad. But when my mom died in 1969 and Casey and I moved to the Majewskis, there was a sense that the Dinges Boys needed to be corralled.

On the first day of fifth grade, right after had we been assigned our desks (I was in the front row), Harriett Cholden, my new teacher, said she wanted to speak to me in her office. It was extremely rare for a teacher to risk the potential mayhem of stepping away from the group to deal with an individual student. Parker had small teachers' offices that each had a window looking out at the classroom. So, I walked back there with Mrs. Cholden who, though less than five feet tall, seemed to tower over me. I could see all my classmates peering into the office.

"I've heard about you," Harriett Cholden said to me. "I know all about you. I know your story. You can't fool me."

"What have you heard?" I asked.

"I've heard you can make it extremely difficult for a teacher to do her job. But I'm different," she said.

I said nothing. I felt like I might crap my pants.

"You are about to make a choice that is going to determine how your entire year goes. Are you ready Barnaby?"

I nodded grimly.

"Good year or bad year. Which is it going to be?" she asked. "I can make every day a living hell for you."

And I believed her. As I looked up at that fierce, fully made-up face and bob haircut, I knew I had met my match. I was going to change. I was going to stop fucking around for laughs all the time.

"Good year, Mrs. Cholden. We're going to have a good year."

And we did. Every night I would retreat to my Majewski tower room closet to read and write my ass off, and Casey did the same thing.

Casey and I had a lot of time to study because we were rarely allowed to go out and see friends. On weekends we had to clean the entire house: all four bedrooms and four bathrooms, as well as the well-traveled main areas, and all the dog hair that collected everywhere.

We got good at using vacuum cleaners and toilet brushes, but there seemed no way to get ahead of the housework because

Darlene kept inventing new projects. One Saturday, we had cleaned the whole house by about 4:00 pm, and we thought we might be able to sneak out to the park when Darlene announced: "I want you to build a compost heap in the backyard for all the dog crap."

Now, imagine a small fenced all-brick area in which two large dogs did several major craps each day for years. It smelled like a horse barn back there. You could smell it from the front of the house when the wind pushed the vapors down the gangway toward the street. We asked how we were going to build this crap compost. "Alan got an enzyme kit at the hardware store. Read the directions and get it done."

The Majewski backyard, where no humans ever trod, was home to an old abandoned sewer, so the plan was to take the heavy iron cover off it and build a brick barrier so that we could toss craps down into the big hole, sprinkle some enzyme on top, and put the lid back on. It took us a few hours with thick rubber gloves on just to gather all the Tango and Billy turds and drop them in the hole, and then another hour to build the brick wall to accommodate future dog droppings. By the time we tossed the enzyme on top and dropped the lid, the sun was down and all we wanted to do was puke.

Life Is Loss

I had a lot of time to think in the Majewski house. I wish I could say I used the time to cultivate great thoughts or weave exotic fantasies. I didn't. I tried to find ways to make time pass more quickly so that the days ended sooner and with less pain. I concentrated on survival, developing mind tricks to pass the time.

I was stuck in the house. There was nothing I wanted to do there, no room where I felt comfortable, no one I really wanted to talk to except my brother. We were often marooned next to each other in our upstairs confinement. I would look out of the irregular-angled front windows on the third floor down at Roslyn Place, and what I saw was a world that made very little sense. Who took my parents away? They must be somewhere. I never saw their bodies in coffins. Could their disappearance be part of some grand hoax? Did the CIA kidnap them to use their talents as part of some great freedom-fighting mission? When are they coming back?

I would sometimes be walking down Clark Street to or from school behind a man or woman who I thought for sure was my mom or dad. But running in front to get a better look, I was always disappointed.

Why did our parents not say goodbye? Dad knew he was dying for years. Why didn't he use the "Fleet of Feet" visit to say goodbye? Too painful? I guess parents don't say goodbye to their children. I concluded the planet is a place where disaster will come visit, and I needed to be ready.

Life is loss. Deal with it. Recognize it. Embrace it because loss is coming. Never rest. Always stay alert. Most important, stay strong—my one-word life motto: STRONG!

I could not wait for Mondays to roll around, to get out of that house to enjoy some fresh air and the freedom of the sidewalk. The four-block walk down Clark Street to and from school was always an adventure, and it attracted all types of humanity.

One afternoon, I was about to turn off Clark onto Roslyn when a tall black woman wearing platform shoes, a big wig, and very little clothing approached me and asked, "Do you want a date? Do you want to have a good time?"

I just stood there, stunned. "I got homework," I said.

"It won't take long. Do you have any money?" she asked.

Over her shoulder, I saw a big black guy across the street standing in front of a dark green Cadillac, watching us closely.

"I spent it on lunch," I said as I tried to step around her and get home. But she followed me.

"I just need one more trick today and then I'm done," she pleaded.

I took off running down Roslyn Place and set my fifth grade record for the 50-yard dash. Seldom had I been so happy to arrive at the Majewski household. I hustled upstairs, toweled off with a washcloth, and got to my homework.

Freedom Games

It would not take much for Darlene to ground me and Casey for weeks, if not a month. A major dog crap or puddle of pee in the house would usually get us a week. Any second-guessing of her labor demands would get us more time in home detention. Casey responded to this by sneaking out at night, tiptoeing down the stairs and slipping out through a basement door under the front stairwell. It wasn't a bad strategy, because we had no dealings with Darlene after we did the dishes and went upstairs each evening and Darlene rarely bothered to climb the stairs to the third floor. But I tried a different approach to gain temporary freedom.

It would usually happen on a weekend evening. Darlene enjoyed playing cards and other games, and she liked to drink Scotch poured from a glass jug that sat on the dining room table (which was used more for poker games than dining). Darlene liked to play Yahtzee, a game with five dice and a scoring sheet that required a good understanding of poker. The player who secured certain combinations was the winner and got to yell, "YAHTZEE!"

I'd ask Darlene if she wanted to play a few games, and we'd sit at the far end of the kitchen table. I'd get her a Scotch on the rocks, and the game would begin. While Darlene was playing to win, I was playing to get her in a congenial frame of mind to let me go visit with a friend. I would stare at her across the table, observing the way her head would bobble slowly back and forth, almost as if she was at sea.

While she was focusing on the dice, I was also fixed on her drink, and how our game progressed. There was an art to my approach: I needed to make it competitive but not win. I needed to make the game last, but not too long. I need her to have a second Scotch, and maybe a third, because I had a question I needed to ask her, but the situation needed to be just right.

The ideal scenario would be that we each won a game and were playing the rubber match for the evening's honors. I didn't care if I won; I really didn't want to. I just wanted to get out of the house for a few hours and feel like a normal kid. When we finished playing, after about an hour, I'd ask, "Can I go out for a little while and visit a friend?"

Darlene would never answer quickly. She would make my fate twist on her whimsy. She'd stare back at me, head titled to one side. It was almost as if a coin was flipping inside her head, but the odds always felt like less than 50 percent. The usual answer would be "not tonight," and I'd beat it up the back stairs to bed. But every so often, a Mitzvah would come my way and Darlene would grant me an evening pass. If I got the green light, I'd run out the front door as fast as I could so she wouldn't have the chance to change her mind.

That mind game went on for years, well into high school. If I was lucky enough to get out, I had to be home by 9:00 pm. The

Majewski kids had no curfew. They had no limits on anything. Separate and unequal was the law of the land.

Casey started sneaking out in middle school. This made me nervous, but I was glad he was getting out. There were a few girls he liked, and he'd sneak out through the basement to go visit them for a few hours. Often, I'd be up in our little room alone.

One evening, I got my homework done and didn't want to venture back downstairs, so I started exploring in Casey's desk. I opened the top drawer and found a sealed envelope. I shook it and heard small bits rolling around inside. I felt compelled to open the envelope to see its contents. I gently opened it and inside I saw some seeds and buds. My hands shook as I held the envelope. What was my brother doing with pot? A seventh grader was too young for that. In a panic, I opened the third floor window off the gangway, lit the envelope on fire with a match, and dropped the burning contents into the gangway. I felt sick as I turned the lights off and got into bed.

When Casey returned to our room, I told him I had something to share. "I found your pot," I said.

"What are you talking about?"

"I found the envelope in your drawer with the marijuana."

"You need to stay out of my shit."

"I didn't want you to use the drugs, so I threw them out."

"What the fuck are you talking about? What did you do, Bar?"

At this point, Casey was standing over the bed glaring down at me.

"I lit the envelope on fire and threw it out the window."

Casey jumped on top of me in bed, and his fists rained down on me. Then he suddenly stopped, grabbed me by the collar, put his face just inches from mine and said, "You dumb little motherfucker. The cops are going to find that envelope and arrest the both of us."

I apologized, but it didn't matter. Och had struck again.

But this time with righteous purpose. We never smoked pot in that house.

Camp Ketchua

It could not have been easy raising five boisterous boys under one roof. As lax a mom as Darlene was, and as absent a father as Alan was, even they needed a break from parenting every so often.

Two years into our stay in the Majewski house, it was announced that the five boys would be shipped off for a month to a sleepover summer camp at Camp Ketchua in northern Michigan. The sprawling camp was located off the shores of Lake Michigamme, which derived its name from the Native American word for "large lake."

It was a woodsy compound with an old freight rail track running nearby. The campers were divided into groups of four and housed in large tan tents that gave it a military feel. Each camper got a metal cot with an elaborate mosquito net that made the tents look like a TB sanitarium from the inside. All meals were eaten at a big wooden lodge that sounded like a sports arena once all the kids got inside.

The camp was very sports oriented and extremely competitive. They had tournaments for everything from tetherball to tennis. Ron Majewski, though he was nowhere near the oldest or biggest kid at the camp, won them all. His form wasn't very good, but he found a way to win at everything with his ruthless will. When he won the badminton tournament, beating the son of the camp owner—who was supposed to be some kind of badminton savant—a fight ensued, and the other kid cracked Ron on the head with his aluminum racket, bending it into a perfect right angle. Ron was unfazed. Suffice it to say, all the Majewski kids (though Ron was the instigator) developed quite a reputation at camp, and I was very happy to be named Dinges.

My problem was I couldn't swim. The camp elders told Darlene and Alan they would teach me how during my month in Michigan. I'm not sure whether it was because I didn't like the water or was terrified by seeing my dad disappearing into large bodies of water wearing his snorkel, or just that I was weak as shit, but I had bad technique. I could tread water for less than a minute before I would tire and start to sink. It was embarrassing.

So, while all the other kids were off on sailboats and swinging off rope tires into the lake, I was at the end of a lonely dock getting tutored by a pissed-off counselor. He would make me jump into the water and dog paddle in place for at least a minute. If I tried to grab the dock, he'd stomp on my fingers and yell at me to stay in the water and keep swimming. This went on for weeks, until near the end of camp, but I could only go five minutes, but this was enough to earn me the right to wear a life jacket and go on the boats with the other kids. I also got the "Most Improved Swimmer" plaque at the end of camp … which felt more like a sympathy gesture, like the gifts my classmates gave me after my dad died. But Casey was proud of me, and that was the real reward.

My bed was my favorite place at camp. I liked to curl up in my little cot, protected from the monstrous mosquitoes, hundreds of miles from the mayhem that was the Majewski household. I felt safe. And I was surrounded by a cast of interesting characters. My cabin included Dick Darling, Toby Douglas, and John Stroh.

Dick Darling was a big fat teddy bear of a kid who cried himself to sleep every night because he missed his mommy and daddy. It was a sad spectacle because his weeping could be heard many tents away, and the older kids would always yell unkind words, like, "Shut the fuck up, you pussy!" Toby Douglas was a fearless and energetic kid who could out "Och" me. He was one of those cute kids that looked like an angel with his blond hair and blue eyes ... but he had the brain of a devil. John Stroh was a slow-talking kid from Detroit, who insisted his family owned a brewery. I told him no one had ever heard of Stroh's beer, and that he was a liar.

One day in the final week of camp, Toby asked if I wanted to take a hike before dinner. We had about 30 minutes, and he said there was a frog pond nearby he wanted to show me. That sounded cool. But walking in the woods with Toby made me nervous; he seemed like the kind of kid that would tie you to a tree and leave you to be devoured my mosquitoes. But I said yes because I really wanted to see some frogs.

We walked a few hundred yards through the woods to the pond and, sure enough, there were frogs everywhere. Big ones ... the size of baseballs. Many frogs were just lined up on fallen logs catching some late afternoon sun. "Watch this," Toby said as he snuck up behind a big frog, grabbed it from the back, and then threw it into the base of a tree. The frog lay on the ground, legs quivering.

"Is it dead?" I asked.

"No, it's just stunned."

Toby then grabbed about ten more big frogs and rifled them off the base of the tree, leaving a pile of them twitching on the ground.

I was speechless at what I was witnessing. He then gathered up the frogs and placed them stomach down on the nearby railroad track, lining them up like a frog train. A few minutes later a freight train rumbled by ... and all that was left of the frogs were their legs lined up on each side of the track. Needless to say, I had very little to eat for dinner that night and was spooked as I went to bed.

The next morning, a few of the counselors took a sunrise walk down to the tracks to put nickels down to get flattened by a train and they discovered the frog massacre. They shared the chilling news at breakfast that morning, and they demanded to know who had done the evil deed. I was staring right across the table at Toby Douglas and was about to stand up and finger him when Toby jumped up and beat me to it, saying: "Barnaby Dinges did it!"

There was an audible gasp in the dining room. Though I had done a lot of bad things in life up to that point, I'd actually been on my best behavior at camp. And I was like the camp mascot, so when Toby launched his charge, I was given the benefit of the doubt.

I learned then that REPUTATION MATTERS! After a brief investigation by the camp elders, I was exonerated and Toby Douglas was sent home. For once, justice had prevailed in my life.

1971

AFTER NEARLY TWO YEARS, the construction project at Roslyn Place was finally complete. I knew nothing about interior design, but it seemed utilitarian at best. A half floor was added to the third floor, and that was handy because it meant all five boys could live up there. Large closets were built out from the walls upstairs, effectively shrinking the rooms but giving us a place to hide our stuff. But the old brownstone looked funny with all its plaster walls covered over by light-brown wood paneling. One could only wonder what was being hidden behind those walls.

Under the new configuration on the third floor, Doug and Mark shared the new addition, Ron got a large room to himself in the middle, and Casey and I shared a larger space at the north end of the house overlooking the street. Alan must have found a sale at an office equipment warehouse because we were all given huge metal desks, featuring three times more surface area than the previous wooden models. The desktops rested on small filing cabinets to the left and right.

As part of the household rejigging, the Majewskis decided to upgrade the aquarium downstairs, and I asked if I could have the small, old one since they were throwing it out. It was a ten-gallon tank, easily big enough for a dozen fish. I had saved a few dollars doing odd jobs for neighbors, just enough to be able to walk down Clark Street and buy a few neon tetras and common guppies. I placed the aquarium right in the middle of my desk so that I could always see it in the background as I did my schoolwork.

I would just get lost watching the fish. I admired the way they swam around independently and would sometimes join up and form schools and swim in unison. Their world was their ten-gallon tank, and they seemed to enjoy it. I was looking after them. But who was looking after me? I began to feel as constrained in the Majewski house as the fish did in the tank. I was restless for a 12-year-old's fun.

King of the Rooftops

As part of the Roslyn home addition, the Majewskis built a simple wood-frame staircase up to the roof, with a skylight that opened to what would become a rooftop garden for parties. One evening, I quietly and gently opened the plastic and aluminum skylight to get onto the roof. Once up there I realized that, because all the homes were connected, I could head east by hopping over roofs and get almost down to the end of the block. Heading in the other direction was trickier because the only access to the roofs was via an old rickety fire escape off the back of a six-flat in the middle of the block. These were tar roofs with many wires and TV antennae and other debris, so agility and concentration were essential skills for successful roof running.

Climbing up to the roof opened a whole new world. Though I was still mostly confined to the house, the roof always afforded adventure. One Saturday, I went up there and tiptoed to the east and saw a girl about my age in one of the backyards reclining on a lawn chair and sunning herself in a white bikini. Her family had just moved into the neighborhood from the suburbs. Her name was Erin, and she was the most stunning creature I'd ever seen. She had straight brown hair down to her shoulders, parted in the middle, and her body was lean and athletic. I was in love, instantly.

I watched Erin for hours as she drank lemonade, sunned herself, and read her teen magazines. Every so often, her mom, Cindy, who had been a fashion model before having kids, came out to check on Erin and offer her something. At some point, Erin looked skyward at a bird, and I fell backwards onto the roof. Did she see me? Had I blown my cover? I needed to be more careful up on the roof.

After a while, I got bored of just looking at things from up there. One Saturday night, yearning for adventure, I snuck down to the kitchen and grabbed two eggs from the refrigerator. I deftly climbed up to the roof and headed east toward the park. There, about 100 feet away on the park sidewalk, I saw a man and a woman who had stopped to talk while walking their dogs.

Hmmm. Can I throw an egg that far? I stepped back a few feet and readied my best Tom Seaver fastball, but the force of my throw caused the egg to break in my hand as I tried to release it. *Shitcakes!* I had just one egg left, and this was my evening's entertainment, so I had to make it count. I decided to go to the hand grenade over-the-shoulder lob. This is when all the nights watching *Combat* with my dad came back to help me because I'd studied how those army dudes lobbed those grenades. Stand up straight, egg grenade in hand, lean down to get the hand down to the right knee, then catapult over your head and release at full extension. The beauty of this technique was it added another ten feet to the drop distance and enabled me to step back and admire the flight of the projectile.

I achieved surprisingly good distance. The egg fell out of the sky near the dog walkers, and the dogs went nuts. You'd have thought the Vietnam War had re-started in Lincoln Park. Dogs and their walkers were freaked out and had no idea where that egg had come from.

I danced weightlessly back home over the rooftops, rinsed off the egg bits, and tucked myself into bed with my heart racing in a combination of joy and mild regret. Why did I egg those innocent people? Will their dogs be traumatized by the pavement bombing? I needed to find a better target.

A few weeks later, I got the courage to go west over the roofs with a dozen eggs. Stepping out of the Majewski house silently through the basement door below the entry stairway, I made my way up the rusty fire escape of a neighboring building.

Once atop the roofs heading west, I needed my best form for this daring mission. The Chicago Bears had a running back named Gayle Sayers—The Kansas Comet—and I greatly admired his running style. No one could touch Sayers when he was running with the football; he'd scored six touchdowns in one game as a rookie.

I put the eggs in my right arm, running-back style, and ran west, announcing the whole thing in my head ("Sayers steps over one defender, hurtles another, leaps into the end zone! Touchdown Bears!"). It was about 9:00 pm on a Saturday night, and Clark Street was jumping. It was a warm evening, so couples were walking hand in hand, and cars were moving slowly through traffic.

I saw the pimp dude with his big green Cadillac parked right across the street. He was leaning on the driver's side door listening to music and having a smoke. He wore a shiny green suit with a matching hat. It was as if the movie *Shaft* was shooting on the North Side of Chicago. I watched him for a few minutes. Every so often he would take a few steps from his car and yell some obscenities at the girls working for him. He seemed like a very mean man, and I felt like doing a very good deed.

I waited until "Shaft" was leaning back comfortably on his ride. I then placed the dozen eggs on a waist-high ledge. Turning my body perpendicular to the street, I grabbed the first egg and lobbed it about 50 feet across the street. It crashed on the street corner five feet in front of the pimp, sending egg splatter flying onto his shoes and pants. "What the fuck?" I heard him yell. He looked around confused.

About ten seconds later, I lobbed number two, gave it a little more air, and it crashed down onto the hood of his car. "Oh hell no, motherfucker!" he yelled as he twirled around looking for where the eggs had come from.

It was time for the big finish, fireworks style. I grabbed the eggs two at a time and lobbed them every five seconds, so that every few seconds a new egg came crashing down. In less than a minute, I'd landed eight eggs on the roof of the Caddy. Both the car and the pimp were an egg-shelled mess, and the dude was going nuts screaming at the sky.

I could have retreated, but I stayed rooted on the rooftop, three stories up across the street, illuminated by the city's strong streetlights. The pimp got a look at me through the haze and pointed in my direction. "I'm going to kill your fucking little white ass," he yelled. "You will die for this!"

My return trip eastward over the rooftops was carefree. I'd shed the dozen eggs, so my hands were free, and I had victory adrenaline coursing through my veins.

As I crept back into the house, I'd never felt so accomplished. I was drenched in sweat. I savored my conquest as I curled up wet, heart still racing, and imagined the pimp going door to door on Roslyn asking white families if they had any little boys he could interrogate.

The next morning, Darlene complained about a dozen eggs that were missing, and the next week I noticed the pimp and his girls had moved on. My little egg assault had been wickedly effective, and I was back flying with the angels. I had an added hop in my step as I ran to school in the mornings.

Mean Darlene

I never felt comfortable in the Majewski kitchen. I'd grown used to doing the dishes there and cleaning the counters and the stove. It was a place to be alert, to be ready for anything; but that made it hard to ever relax and enjoy a meal.

One Saturday I was up early enjoying some Kaboom cereal, the type that had so many artificial colorings in it that the milk would turn purple. Yum! Darlene appeared early that day in a short nightgown. She entered the kitchen, opened the refrigerator, bent forward ... and showed me her world from the back side. I saw a gray-haired fleshy mass that turned my stomach immediately. I used the rear stairwell to run to my room to try to unsee all that.

As we got up into middle and high school, Casey and I often had sports practice after school, which delayed our return home. One evening Casey appeared at dinner later than normal, sweating from having run home to join the fray. As he stepped toward the dinner table, Darlene asked, "Have you fed the dogs yet? You're late."

"No, I just got home. Soccer ran late," Casey said.

And with that, Darlene took Casey's plate off the table, filled with a pile of meat mush and potatoes, and put it on the kitchen floor between Tango and Billy, who devoured it instantly.

"If the dogs don't eat, you don't eat," Darlene said. "You can go upstairs and think about what you did."

I followed Casey upstairs soon after and told him I'd sneak him up some snacks after I got done cleaning the dishes.

That night I reflected on the journey Casey and I were on, and how it seemed to be getting tougher, more challenging. I was increasingly aware of a world of friends and fun outside the house, much of which we were missing. Were we so bad? What had we done? We didn't kill our parents. They died, and we were dealing with it. But it seemed we had no time to absorb it. But at least we suffered together, and that seemed to strengthen our bond.

Interestingly, once we were housed at the Majewskis, nobody from the state's child welfare agencies came to check on our health and wellbeing. They figured we were placed in a Lincoln Park house and went to a private school, so everything must be all right.

As I shut my eyes and went to sleep that night, the voice in my head—my voice—would tell me that everything would be okay and to *just get to tomorrow, and then get through tomorrow. One day you will be free to run wherever you want. THIS LIFE is temporary.*

1972

I'm not sure what, if anything, Darlene did when the five boys were at school, but once we got home she would be reliably parked in the far right corner of the kitchen table in the back of the house, with the back door and stove to her right and the sink and refrigerator to her left. She would conduct court from there, keeping an eye on things and barking out orders when necessary. Her presence made me want to avoid the kitchen.

At some point, and I'm not sure whether it was her lack of doing laundry with any regularity, or part of Casey's rebellion, but Darlene became convinced that Casey was not changing his underwear. She accused him of wearing the same pair of gray-white briefs every day. He denied it.

This was vintage Darlene. Pick an innocuous thing to obsess about, make a big deal about it, and get her target to start to question his own sanity. I'm sure there were days when Casey didn't put on new underwear. I knew I had those days, because reliable clothing was not a staple of life in the Majewski house. Darlene's greatest joy was catching Casey or me in a small lie so that she could blow it up to suggest we were flawed to the core. She loved to call us liars; that seemed to make her day.

"You can't even be trusted to change your underwear on a daily basis. What kind of animal are you? Did you grow up in a barn?"

This daughter of a Kosher butcher in Detroit had very high standards.

Darlene's solution to the Great Underwear War of 1972 was to mandate that at 8:00 pm every night, Casey had to present his underwear to her in the kitchen as he manually tossed it down the laundry chute. This mandate was in force even when there was company over, so Casey had to interrupt whatever drunken scene was unfolding in the kitchen for his grand presentation. This gambit by Darlene struck me as particularly cruel and weird, and it made me realize that Casey's rebellious tactics were likely the path I, too, would need to pursue. You humiliate my brother, you humiliate me.

Grappling Ron

Ron Majewski was a year older than me, and Casey was a year older than Ron, meaning when they got into high school, they might compete for some of the same positions on sports teams. Ron was one of those kids that matured early and achieved his full height by his freshman year in high school. This enabled him to physically dominate most of his peers. Ron approached the world like a big, hungry animal. If he wanted something—food, a girl, an opportunity—he took it.

Casey was a gifted but ill-tempered athlete. He was fast, competitive, and determined. He ran with such speed and ferocity that I could hear him panting when he would run nearby.

Casey and Ron had a few skirmishes over the years, and on two occasions I was right in the middle. Once was at summer camp at Francis Parker School. On a rainy day, the boys were all inside playing floor hockey with plastic sticks and pucks. I played goalie because I was quick around the net. Once, I made a save, and Ron, who was on the other team, started slashing wildly for the puck that was in my hands. As I was rolling on the gym floor in agony, Casey jumped on Ron's back, and a full-scale hockey fight ensued.

Another time we were playing Kick the Can in front of the house on Roslyn Place. I was protecting the can from a few feet away when Ron came running up. While I was counting him out with my foot on the can ("One, two, three, I see Ron"), he slid through me on the sidewalk, like Pete Rose barreling through Roy Fosse at home plate in the All-Star Game. Ron's ridiculous slide launched me into the air, and I crashed down on the pavement, scratched, bruised, and dazed. As I looked up, Casey was on Ron again. Casey had my back, and that felt good.

That year, Casey and Ron both tried out for the JV basketball team, competing for the guard position. Ron was a better defender and physical presence, but Casey was a better shooter, passer, and ball handler. It looked like Casey was primed to be a starting guard when Darlene intervened.

Darlene determined that Casey's angry outbursts, both in sports and life, were problematic and needed professional attention. Forget that his parents had died and he was living in an unfriendly foster home … this kid needed to see a shrink. A lot. As many days as possible.

So, Darlene found the most expensive psychotherapist on Michigan Avenue and scheduled Casey to go there three afternoons a week. The visits effectively removed Casey from the JV basketball team AND put a substantial drain on the Dinges boys' holdings. It also effectively ended any hope that Darlene and Casey would be anything other than at war. And as Casey's younger brother, I was deemed an enemy combatant no matter what I did.

Steroid Solution

While my brother was wrong in the head, according to Darlene, my problem was that I was too short. I was so short, she said, that it was affecting my personality, and I was acting out all the time to get attention. In eighth grade, I was four-foot-ten and weighed less than 100 pounds. All the boys in my class were bigger, and most of the girls. I was nowhere near puberty. Darlene decided my size was a detriment, and a danger to my future. She raised three burly boys; my runtiness was unacceptable.

She found the name of a doctor in Skokie specializing in the experimental use of steroids to boost growth in young boys. Every few weeks, I would take the bus for hours out to Skokie to a nondescript brick building off a strip mall where Dr. Steiner would X-ray my joints and report that the window was closing on my ability to grow. The time to start the steroid treatment was NOW. He set me up on a drug called Anavar, an anabolic steroid used to boost muscle mass. It was a new drug and very expensive. It also came with a long list of precautions ("might cause cancer, heart and liver disease, high blood pressure … frequent or ongoing erections, acne"), which I read one day on the bus riding home.

Though I didn't mind bulking up, no one asked me if this was something I wanted to do. I was like a lab rat, an expensive one. Between the visits to Steiner, the X-rays, and the drugs, my treatments rivaled Casey's shrink visits in cost. Between the Roslyn remodeling and our medical bills, Casey and I began to worry whether there would be any money left for college once the Majewskis were finished with it.

Poker & Parties

With five teenage boys living under one roof, and a matriarch who fashioned herself to be one of the great poker players of all time, the house began to take on the feel and aroma of an old Western saloon. Darlene liked to host weekend poker games, attended mostly by Alan's musician friends from the Chicago Symphony Orchestra. These were high stakes games in which hundreds of dollars would change hands, with Darlene usually on the losing end. But she liked to drink Scotch and gamble with the boys, and if an evening cost her $500 in losses (plus the cost of cold cuts and booze), so be it. Alan would just take on a few more harp students or load the harp into the Marathon and go make a few more recordings for commercials.

I would watch the poker games from the top of the second floor stairs, peering down on a large table for eight set up in the middle of the first floor. The Majewski boys were also allowed to host games, and they often would get one going after school. I learned a lot about poker and gambling watching from afar. Darlene would also allow the Majewski kids to drink beer, and their friends as well.

Darlene finished off the rooftop garden with a five-foot-high wooden fence and green plastic fake grass. Though cheaply constructed, it was nice to look out at the sky and surrounding highrises that were going up in the neighborhood. The Majewskis would have an annual Fourth of July party which served as a good way to show off their newly enhanced home, and to make it appear as though the house was a normal place to live.

I liked those parties because there would be so much booze and bedlam flowing that I could sneak off into the neighborhood and return to some of my old haunts for some mayhem of my own. I had a friend called Mit Sanford, whose parents' philosophy was to send him out into the world each day with a few dollars and instructions to have fun, try to learn something, and don't get killed or arrested.

One time, Mit and I snuck away from a Majewski drunk fest to a nearby rubble lot where some homes had been torn down to expand a local hospital. I had an empty thick-glass 64-ounce Coke bottle and Mit had an M80 explosive. We walked to the middle of the lot, put the bottle on the ground, lit the fuse on the M80 and dropped it into the bottle. We then turned and sprinted away from the bottle, and about five seconds later it blew up into a million little glass shards that came falling like little daggers out of the sky and onto our heads. We didn't stop running for about a minute. When we finally stopped, we turned to each other, heaving with sweat and fear, and laughed like the crazy kids we were.

"Mit," I said. "That was the dumbest thing we've ever done."

We slinked back into the party and finished off a few beers that were left unattended.

Sneaky Sleepovers

I liked the rooftop garden because it afforded the opportunity to have a friend sleep over and "escape" the house at the same time. One time, Charlie Farwell came over, and we hauled the heavy sleeping bags up to the roof and laid them out at the north end. Charlie had brought some candy-covered almonds, and we enjoyed these as we looked up at the stars and had one of those forgettable conversations near-teenagers have when they are trying to not sound like idiots.

But after a while, we got tired of talking and munching on the candied almonds and started looking over the fence down to

Roslyn Place, which was typically a very quiet side street. Across the street, up on the second level of the three-story brick building, we could see an old man sitting in a chair reading. Charlie and I looked at each other and knew what was going to happen next. I lobbed a candy across the street, and it bounced off the brick wall not far from the second-floor window. Miss. Charlie tossed one … closer, but another miss.

By about the 20th toss, we were pinging the window with impressive frequency. We saw the old man cup his hands around his eyes to look out the window. No doubt he wondered what was pinging his window. He went back to his chair to continue reading, but our candy assault continued. Our accuracy was hilarious! Ping, ping, ping … we couldn't get enough of our success. After about 30 minutes, a Chicago Police Department squad car pulled up in front of the house, parked in front of the fire hydrant, and two officers came to the Majewski's door.

Holy crap! The old man had narced on us. Charlie and I dove back into our sleeping bags and buried the remaining candy bags by our feet. A few minutes later, the two officers and Darlene opened the squeaky skylight door. Charlie and I pretended to be asleep. The officers came toward us with their flashlights trained on us.

"Do you two know anything about someone using a BB gun to shoot at the windows across the street?"

"No sir, " I said. "We're just camping out up here. We don't have a gun."

At this point the officers instructed us to come out of the sleeping bags, which they held up and shook to make sure no heavy weapon was inside. Darlene knew we were up to something … but I think we had even her confused. She knew there were no guns in the Majewski house.

The police inspected the roof, shining their bright lights into all the dark corners. Finding nothing they came over to give us one last piece of advice. "Stay out of trouble up here … and have a good sleepover."

Charlie and I were silent in our sleeping bags until we heard the patrol car pull away. We giggled quietly at our narrow escape. We thought of resuming the candy war, but talked ourselves out of it. We chuckled at the thought of someone in the morning seeing hundreds of candied almonds strewn over the ground in front of the apartment building across the street.

As I dozed off to sleep in the cool evening air, I wondered if it had been better if the cops had hauled me off. I could tell them I was in a hostage situation, and maybe they'd believe me. I'd be free of Darlene. But that was just a dream.

Casey the Builder

My brother was a meticulous builder, and one day in shop class he took a square piece of Plexiglas and attached it to a wooden frame. We would use this contraption to place over the closets in our bedroom so that we could play Nerf basketball together. Casey was increasingly in a state of perpetual grounding, so we would need to think of ways to entertain ourselves on weekends.

When we were alone in the house, we would place the backboard over the closet, strip down to our undies, and have battles that rivaled anything that happened at the Chicago Stadium. Casey was still bigger and faster than me, but the steroids were starting to kick in, so I at least had some bulk to slow him down. The rim was about six feet high, so I could dunk. We would bounce off each other for hours, landing so hard sometimes the whole house would shake. Though Darlene had not ventured up to the third floor for years, it would only take one heroic climb and our game would be done.

Casey would hide the backboard in the closet so that not even the Majewski boys knew about it. It was our secret, and I liked that.

The Towel Boy

Appearances were important to Darlene and the Majewskis. They wanted to be perceived in the tight Parker School community as a benevolent family that took in two orphan boys despite having three sons of their own. Darlene needed to let us do a few "public" things so she could deny that she made us do constant chores and virtually shackled us for 52 weeks a year. The optics were good. But Casey and I had started to complain to some of our close friends and their parents, and even some trusted friends at school. While the kids were shocked to hear some of the stories we shared, most of the adults said things like, "It can't be that bad." We were lucky the Majewskis took us in, they said, and they told us to "Hang in there—it will get better."

The summer after seventh grade, when most of my friends were going to camp or taking exotic trips with their families, I got a job working as a towel boy at Parker School Summer Camp. I just could not pull myself away from the school that I loved. I was also learning new places to explore.

My job as towel boy required me to retreat to the bowels of the school to a furnace room with blasters the size of small nuclear reactors and a huge old washer and dryer for clothes. There were rats down there and cigarette butts and spent rubbers from the shenanigans that happened in the dark underbelly of any old school.

The camp was for kids from kindergarten to sixth grade, and there were about 14 groups of boys and girls in groups of 15—more than 200 kids total. A big part of the camp, which I'd attended in years past, was to hop on a bus daily and ride 15 minutes to an old, dungeon-like building called Lincoln Turner Pool; you could smell the burn of chlorine in the pool a block away. Because I was a horrible swimmer and always hated going to Lincoln Turner, I'd get sharp pains in my stomach and break out in a rash over much of my body just entering the building. I also witnessed horrible things there, like a kid taking a crap right by the ledge of the pool from fear of the water, and our counselors, who were grown men, toweling their balls for way too long.

I was pleased to be no longer attending that camp and just in charge of the towels instead, working in the hellish heat of the boiler room for $1 per hour. The problem was, the towels just kept on coming and I was dealing with some faulty equipment. My job was to collect the towels throughout the day and have them cleaned, dried, folded, and waiting for each group before they boarded the bus to go swimming. It seemed easy enough, but the washer was slow and lacked vigor, and the huge front-loading dryer rarely generated the heat to dry towels quickly. I soon learned that there was no way to gather all the towels and get them cleaned and folded in time for the swim groups. I needed a workaround. This is when I learned I was a pretty decent problem solver.

I'd collect the towels and sift through them to see which were the most dirty and wet. Those towels I would clean, but the ones that looked mostly white and not too wet, I threw in the dryer immediately to stay ahead of the game. I noticed the girls' towels tended to remain in good shape and smelled nice, whereas the boys' towels often had racing stripes, which caused me to wonder if anyone had taught them how to properly wipe their asses.

My method went along swimmingly until after about a month, when some of the persnickety counselors noticed all the towels appeared to have spots like those on a snow leopard. I was interrogated by the camp elders and insisted I was doing the best

I could. I suggested an investment in bleach, new towels, and new equipment.

Camp ended soon after, and in six weeks, I'd made $240. I banked $200 of it. Being 13, I needed adult supervision to open an account. Alan took me to a local branch bank, but Darlene insisted I could only open a bank account if she cosigned every time I withdrew money. What could have been a proud moment of prudent saving instead felt like my money was locked up and Darlene had the key.

1973

In middle school, I began to listen closely to my teachers, and in sixth grade, I had a stylish young teacher named Mary Beth Berkoff. She had black hair and a curvy mod bod that reminded me of Ali McGraw in that movie, *Love Story*. She was smart and challenging and managed to get our class involved in dynamic conversations. I always participated, in part to duel with my classmates, and in part to impress her. She was mom-like ... at least the kind of mom I wanted at the time. One day, as we were discussing human development, she said, "Studies suggest that most children are a fully formed human being by the age of six. They will develop and change with time, but they are essentially WHO THEY ARE at six." At that point the class continued without me, as I enjoyed a warm feeling inside. Doing the math, I realized that my parents had given me all they could and all I needed. Dad died when I was seven, and Mom died when I was nine. Ricka and Chuck made me and got me beyond age six, so I was going to be just fine. Maybe I wasn't a freak after all.

The Johnsons

The summer after eighth grade, I got a reprieve of sorts. There was a family at Parker, the Johnsons, who were a Midwest version of the Kennedys. They had old money and an outdoor spirit, and they reached out to Darlene directly to see if I might be able to spend a month with them up in Canada at their family compound north of Sault St. Marie. They called it North Camp, and they wanted me to befriend and "babysit" their boisterous son Bradley, who was ten at the time.

Darlene originally said no, but I pleaded with her, especially since they were willing to pay me $100 per week. I could enjoy the fresh air of Canada, get to know Bradley and the Johnson family … and most importantly, get the hell away from Roslyn Place for a few weeks. Darlene relented, I think because the Johnson family was influential at Parker School, and it would have been unreasonable not to let me get out and have this summer experience. Letting me go to Canada would quell some of the talk that all was not well at House Majewski.

The Johnson's North Camp Compound was impressive. Situated on 20 woodsy acres off a huge lake, the property had a main lodge for meals and six cabins for family and staff. There were a lot of people working there, including a caretaker and three people in the kitchen. One of them caught my eye immediately. Her name was Rhonda Tees. She was in her early 20s and helped in the kitchen. She looked like a young Sally Field, with more of an hourglass shape. She had brown hair down to her shoulders, round dimpled cheeks, big brown eyes, and a frequent smile.

I just liked to sit around the kitchen and watch Rhonda work, but Bradley kept me busy. Unlike me, Bradley was a natural outdoorsman and capable around the water. He would take me down to the end of the long dock and, within minutes, we'd snag a huge northern pike for dinner. The family had several vintage powerboats and sailboats, and Bradley could operate them all. We'd get a grocery list from the kitchen staff and hop in a small fishing boat with a rear engine. Bradley would guide us across the lake to shop in town where we would pick up the mail. In many ways it seemed like he was chaperoning *me*.

Bradley was a nice kid, but bored. All his siblings were older, and his parents were tired of parenting. I did my best to be his friend. We shared a cabin together, and before bed and on rainy days, we'd read Hardy Boys books aloud (and Nancy Drew too!). We'd pack lunches and take long hikes in the woods. With his blond locks and innate athleticism, he reminded me of young Tarzan running through the forest.

One weekend, Mr. Jensen Johnson arrived from his important job in Washington, DC. That Saturday, the entire Johnson family and I boarded their big sailboat for a ride out into the channels near their property. Jensen Johnson was one of those larger-than-life Americans: handsome, gritty, and smart. He looked like a young Robert Redford, and I believed he could do anything. The way he rigged the huge sails on the boat and guided it out into the water felt like we controlled the water and the wind.

We sailed for hours until we came upon a small uninhabited island, where we dropped anchor and carried our lunch onto shore. It felt strange, this combination of freedom and happiness. There was a big great world out there to explore, and one day I would find a way to experience it. Just not now. Not while Darlene Majewski controlled my fate.

Help Me, Rhonda

Bradley was my job, but Rhonda was my passion. I thought about her constantly and always tried to find a way to linger in a room when she was there. We didn't talk much until one rainy afternoon. As she was skinning potatoes, I blurted out awkwardly, "Do you have a boyfriend?"

She looked at me, blushed, and then answered. "Yes, I'm

dating a hockey player. But I hardly ever see him because he's always practicing or traveling. He hopes to play in the NHL someday."

Well, I knew I couldn't compete with a hockey stud ... but I could help his girl laugh and enjoy her summer. From then on, Rhonda and I talked all the time. One evening she even invited me down to the dock for a sunset swim, and she arrived in a white dimply bikini that highlighted her summer tan and perfect body. It took my entire brainpower not to get an erection that I would have no idea how to disguise. Thank God for cold water.

When we got out of the water, her form was even more perfect and taut, and I could see the dark outlines of her nipples through her bikini top. I was becoming a young man, and it was exciting. I started to think about her at night when I went to sleep, and she was still on my mind when I awoke in the morning. I felt passionate love for the first time.

Not long after the swim, we were in the kitchen talking. We were seated at a side table, and I was helping her clean and cut green beans. We were looking out the window together and noticed two squirrels not getting along. One appeared to be trying to mount the other from behind, and the one in front kept turning to fight the other one off.

"I wonder what's going on there," Rhonda said.

After a pause I responded, "Maybe those squirrels are incompatible."

Rhonda smiled at me and laughed from deep inside. "Barnaby, you just used a word I don't think my boyfriend would even understand."

I smiled back at her. Maybe she loved me back. Rhonda was coming around my way. Score!

With about a week left in the summer, when Bradley was off on his own, I decided to do a little exploring. Everyone seemed occupied in the lodge kitchen, so I stepped carefully over to Rhonda's cabin for a look inside. Her cabin was very neat, with a novel by her nightstand and letter-writing paper on her desk.

I moved over to the dresser and, opening the top drawer, saw her bras and panties. Jackpot! They were all so soft, made of cotton and mesh and the lightest gossamers imaginable, mostly whites and some pastels. I reached in, grabbed two handfuls of panties, and was about to caress my face with them when I heard the cabin's screen door squeak open.

"What are you doing in my cabin?" Rhonda asked, not smiling.

I was stunned and sick to my stomach. "I was just looking around," I said weakly.

"Well, these are my things, and you should not be in here."

"I'm sorry," I said as I ran past her and into the woods.

When I got a few hundred yards into the forest, I stopped and got down on my knees and cried the tears of a young boy who had just ruined his dream. I mourned the loss of Rhonda and her trust. I ruined a blooming relationship. What was wrong with me? Was I a pervert? Could I blame this on the Majewskis? Had they denied me so much normal socialization that I didn't know how to act properly? I sat there for a long while, hating myself, and concluded this one was on me. Och was back on the Ming Trail. I had to own this one.

I avoided Rhonda for the rest of the Canada trip and wrote her a letter of apology when I got back to Chicago, expressing sorrow for destroying our friendship. She wrote me back and said not to worry, she understood. Darlene had, of course, opened my mail and asked me: "Who is this Rhonda and what did you do to her?"

"Just a girl I met in Canada, a friend," I told Darlene.

"Well, no girlfriends for you, not for a very long time," Darlene commanded.

My traditional summer fun was limited to a week I got to head north to visit my friend Charlie at his family cabin off Green Bay, Wisconsin. I'd get there via a day-long ride on a Greyhound Bus, which turned a five-hour drive into a nine-hour slog. Waukegan, Kenosha, Sheboygan, Manitowoc, Sturgeon Bay, Fish Creek … it would take forever to get to Door County from Chicago. But as sweaty and stinky as the Greyhound Bus was, it was a relief to be free and clear of the Majewskis, and to spend a week with the Farwells, who seemed to genuinely like their kids and know how to have a good time.

Door County was the Midwest version of Cape Cod, with its fried seafood and tacky gift shops. A small peninsula with Lake Michigan on one side and Green Bay on the other, water was everywhere, and the sunrises and sunsets were spectacular, even for a kid.

Crab Apples

Charlie was good at everything, and he had almost everything: a go cart and a little motorcycle, too. He knew how to play pool and captain boats. He seemed to glide through life with an ease fed by talent and good upbringing. We couldn't drive yet, but Door County was the type of place people hitchhiked around, and Charlie's mom, Carol, let us do that, thinking it would help us grow up and learn to be independent. I appreciated Carol's faith in us; parental confidence was unfamiliar.

One evening we decided to meet up with two of Charlie's friends, Ted and Ozzie, in Fish Creek. They were from rich families and spent the whole summer in Door County, as did Charlie. After getting bored hanging out downtown with no young girls to talk to, we decided to gather up a few buckets of crab apples and go find some worthy targets. Tired of throwing apples at each other and unlucky squirrels and rabbits, we ended up in a driveway at the end of a sharp turn as traffic came into town. It was a perfect spot because the driveway was secluded and we could watch cars coming down the hill after descending the bluff on Highway 42, their headlights sweeping through the woods along the road. We decided to splatter the next car we saw, so we each grabbed a handful of crab apples and lined up in a row in the driveway.

Soon after, a car came rolling down the hill and coasted into the sharp right turn. As it cleared the driveway trees, we all heaved our apples in unison. But right before release, I noticed the car said "Sheriff" on the side and the driver had his window halfway down. I heard about ten apples shotgun the driver's side, and I swear I heard an apple hit the officer's temple, causing a loud groan.

The vehicle slammed on its brakes and sent gravel flying everywhere. My three partners in crime hauled ass up the hill and back into town, but I was frozen for a second. By the time I turned to get up the hill, the cop car was turning into the driveway, and I seemed to spin my wheels as I tried to climb the hill, which was made of large, sharp black rocks. I got about halfway up the hill and ducked behind a tree that was maybe two inches wider than me.

The officer parked in the driveway and swung his bright searchlight back and forth past my head. "I'm gonna find you little fuckers, and when I do, you're dead," the officer yelled. "I got all fucking night. I'm gonna sit here until you come out." The lights from his vehicle cast a long shadow into the woods, and there was a flashing red light too, either from his car or the stop sign at the base of the hill. Every few minutes he would get the spotlight out and scan the woods, and I swear the spotlight settled a few times on the tree I hid behind. It felt like a laser on the back of my neck. I was heaving with fear and sweating. I tried to be still, since a minor movement could jostle all the loose rocks around me. This felt like the end.

I seemed to fall into a motionless trance as I reflected on my journey from losing my parents to the Majewski's hazing. And I would be the bad guy, the scoundrel, the juvenile delinquent. Dispatched to Door County for a week, I attacked the local police. I'd surely go to jail for this, if the officer didn't beat me to death first. I'd squandered all the love and opportunities that had been extended to me by the Parker School community. I prayed to the heavens for forgiveness, but I heard and felt nothing in return. I was a bad kid who deserved a bad ending. Hours passed, the red light kept flashing below, and I must have fallen asleep in my sorrow.

Then I heard: "Dinges, where are you? It's safe. Come on out."

It was Charlie and the gang. I came down the hill looking like a coal miner at the end of a long day. We laughed about our misguided attack on the Sheriff. I didn't admit the terror I felt, but after a few minutes of loitering in the offending driveway, I suggested: "Let's get out of here. This place gives me the creeps."

A Dog's Life

The County Fair was a Parker School tradition—an all-school, day-long celebration where each grade took on a traditional role. Eighth Grade put on a play suitable for the lower grades, and in 1973 we put on *The Wizard of Oz*. I loved that film. I identified with the Munchkins due to their diminutive size, and the "Somewhere Over the Rainbow" song always gave me chills because I dreamed I'd see my parents again in heaven one day.

The role of Dorothy went to Alice Pleasance, the tall, slim, blonde daughter of a great ballerina mom and an industrialist father. Alice could sing and dance and was perfect for the part.

I pined to be the Scarecrow, but was given the non-speaking role of Toto because the drama teachers figured I'd run around and make hay with the role. And, boy, were they right. It helped that they rented me this cool faux fur full-body suit and painted a little brown nose and whiskers on my face so that I could own being a Cairn Terrier. I was totally Toto.

Because we were putting on a show for kindergarten through seventh graders, I suggested that it'd be funny—and realistic—if Toto could lift his leg a half dozen times or so during the show, just to get a few laughs and keep the audience engaged. So, whenever I sensed a lull in the show, I'd pretend to pee while I was on all fours … and the kids in the audience squealed with delight.

I felt like I owned their eyeballs. Without uttering a word, I nearly stole the show. It helped that the show's choreography called for a lot of running, so when Toto was getting chased by the flying monkeys, I leapt from the stage into an aisle and ran out of the auditorium, only to run back in seconds later, down the other aisle toward the stage. The audience cheered as I jumped back onto the stage and climbed a series of risers to look down at the monkeys and the amped-up audience. Sweat poured off my body and into the rented fur suit.

The revved-up audience got me a little carried away, and when Alice was singing her big rainbow number, I ambled over to her and lifted my leg, eliciting a combination of laughter from the kids and groans from some of the adults in the audience.

The show was well received, and I was exhilarated by the experience as I returned home that evening. Darlene, who'd seen the show, was not laughing.

"What were you thinking?" she asked. "Lifting your leg all over the place. That was disgusting."

"It was a kids' show," I responded. "And they loved it."

"Nobody liked it," Darlene said. "You embarrassed the entire family. I don't want to even look at your face. Go to your room and think about all the people you need to apologize to."

I apologized to Alice the next morning, but that was about it.

1974

Darlene was prescient when she predicted it would be a long time before I had a girlfriend. While she was talking about all the barriers and prohibitions she would put in my way, I brought some of my own limits to the party.

As I started freshman year at Francis Parker School, in addition to being under five feet tall, the steroids Darlene hoisted on me caused terrible acne on my face and back. Luckily my locker was in a dark corner of the high school corridor, so I could avoid visibility in the main hallway. My confidence was so low that the only girl I talked to was Atalia Avriel, a blue-eyed Israeli exchange student with a bowl haircut. Her dad was the Israeli Ambassador to Chicago. Tali (as we called her) was new to the US, and her English was not great. I imagined she was like my mom had been as a teenager: exotic in appearance with a choppy command of the English language.

My low self-esteem also was fed by an awkward FWP practice where, starting in eighth grade, the boys were forced to shower together in a big open stall with eight shower heads mounted around a u-shaped wall. The showering part wasn't so bad ... it was getting to and from the shower without the other boys seeing your manly parts (or in my case, underdeveloped boyish bits). At age 14, some boys had massive shlongs wrapped in full pubic plumage. And there were kids like me, who weren't even getting started. It was a mortifying experience, and though there was no name calling at the time, I could only imagine the ripe content the shower exposures created for the robust Parker gossip mill.

Afraid of girls and completely unprepared to even approach them, I buried myself in academics and sports. Every day was the same: wake up early, quick breakfast, run to school, study in library, participate in classes, sports practice after school, run home, quick dinner, clean kitchen, study at my desk upstairs, finally go to sleep, and wake up the next day to do the same thing all over again. The routine was comforting, and it seemed to take the edge off the Majewski oppression. Every day I was getting older and a day closer to being on my own someday. I just had to get there.

Frederick Lazar

As winter break approached, I dreaded the Majewski holiday non-traditions ... but then another mitzvah came my way. I had a new friend named Frederick Lazar, whose father, Louis, owned a bank in downtown Chicago. I had never heard of a family owning a bank. Frederick's family had a fancy apartment off the Mag Mile in Chicago, and they had a yacht parked in Burnham Harbor off downtown, where a grizzled navy vet named Jack captained the vessel and lived on it full time.

Frederick and I started hanging out, and his dad reached out to Darlene directly to say he thought I had potential and he wanted to help me succeed. Darlene liked the status of having a bank president seek her association. The relationship was further cemented when Darlene would have dinner parties at which Frederick and I, wearing black bowties and white dress shirts, served her guests and then cleaned all the dishes for the grand total of $2 each. I was amused that the son of a bank president would work five hours for $2 just to be my friend, but it showed a commitment that I appreciated. I knew Frederick and I would do great things together.

In early December, Louis Lazar called Darlene and asked if I could join the Lazar family for their annual holiday trip to the Fontainebleau Hotel in Miami. The trip would last about a week, and they would teach me how to play tennis and go deep-sea fishing. Darlene originally said no—"I hadn't earned the privilege of such a trip"—but Louis Lazar persisted. Darlene finally said yes, but only if I paid my own way using estate funds. Louis Lazar was insulted by Darlene's pettiness, but he agreed.

The Lazars were one of those Jewish families, like many at Parker, in which lively chatter and probing questions were the norm. Louis and his wife, Lara, were keenly interested in all aspects of our freshman lives—what we were studying, who the hot girls at school were, who the biggest asshole in our class was. I cherished being with them, even for just a week, and they gave me a sense of what being with a loving, engaged family could feel like.

On most days, Louis and Frederick would go off for a tennis lesson and I would lie by the pool with Lara, who wore a white bikini that made me think of Rhonda … and Lara's 40-something body was reminiscent as well. Lara would order me cheeseburgers, and the cabana boy would bring us some cold Cokes every 30 minutes. After a few days, however, the routine was getting boring. Thankfully, Frederick said his relative had called and asked if we wanted to get together with some girls. That sounded great. My tan had covered up most of my zits, and the thought of meeting some Miami girls and enjoying some McDonald's burgers and fries in the warm evening air sounded fantastic.

*Casey and I charge into Lake Michigan at a beach
in north Chicago in the early 1960s.*

Ricka's beauty is on full display in this formal sorority shot from Michigan State University in the early 1950s.

The stress, strain, and intensity of illness are evident in the face of Chuck Dinges, who sat for this business headshot in the mid-1960s.

Chuck and Ricka taking a break on a piano bench on their wedding night in the early 1950s.

A family classic: the Dinges foursome pause in a Chicago alley in the early 1960s.

Hans and Yulick Leonhardt, Ricka's parents, enjoying an intimate but formal moment together in East Lansing, Michigan, where they both worked as professors at Michigan State University.

Casey and I take turns "riding" Chuck's motorcycle, parked out in front of our first-floor apartment on Wrightwood Avenue in Chicago's Lincoln Park neighborhood in the early 1960s.

Casey and I display baseball antics during a visit to Grandmother's house in East Lansing, after Chuck's death in 1966.

Chuck enjoys taking his sons out for a weekend drive in a classic VW bug in 1961.

Casey and I clown around on the sidewalk in downtown Chicago during an office visit with Chuck, a rising star at an ad agency in the early 1960s.

Casey and me dressed up in formal wear for an outing with our grandmother in 1961.

Hans Leonhardt, revered professor, enjoys a father-daughter moment with Ricka at the beach in the late 1950s.

Chuck manifests his kinetic energy in his ad executive "uniform" downtown in the mid-1960s.

Ricka strikes a pensive pose in her writing office at the family apartment on Wrightwood Avenue in the mid-1960s.

I sport a Beatles-style haircut in front of the small patch of grass between three-flat apartment buildings on Wrightwood Avenue in Chicago in the mid-1960s.

Ricka wearing a somber expression for this photo with me and Casey during a trip to Jamaica in 1965, the last family trip before Chuck died in 1966.

Ricka and Yulick enjoying a mother-daughter moment in the 1950s.

Students at MSU, Chuck and Ricka, heading out on their first date in East Lansing in the early 1950s. Note the contrasting fashion sensibilities.

Professor Yulick Leonhardt, Ricka's mother, on her way to teach a German language class at MSU in East Lansing in the 1950s.

I look down with pride after conquering Dunn's River Falls in Ocho Rios, Jamaica, in 1965 during the family's last trip as a foursome.

Close friend Charlie Farwell and I pause on the playground at Francis W. Parker School while in kindergarten in 1964. Note Charlie's stylish look and and my clothes from the Jimmy Hoffa Collection.

I hoist a big Rainbow Trout I caught in Canada and celebrate with a Fanta root beer while working as a babysitter for the Johnson family in 1973.

I show off a crew cut during a visit to Lincoln Park in the 1960s.

Casey and I don cowboy hats and skin-tight swimsuits for a blackmail-worthy photo from the early 1960s.

I display disdain for cats during a family outing to rural Illinois in 1966.

Ricka strikes an elegant pose in a mysterious photo from the mid-1960s.

Ricka looking young and carefree with bangs and a stylish turtleneck in a headshot from the late 1950s.

A young Chuck Dinges stands out among his elder peers while judging ad campaigns for an awards ceremony in the early 1960s.

Promotional piece touting Professor Hans Leonhardt's national speaking tour on International Relations. A maritime lawyer from Danzig, Germany, Hans wrote an influential book called Nazi Conquest of Danzig *and toured the U.S. talking to business and foreign relations groups about the future of post-Hitler Europe.*

I strike a fierce pose in the early 1960s, sporting the crew cut Chuck passed onto his boys following his U.S. Army service during the Korean War.

Chuck enjoying a business-casual moment in the mid-1960s; his thinning hair and waistline were early signs of the leukemia that would slowly take his life during a five-year illness that was first diagnosed in 1961.

Chuck yucking it up with his secretary during a photo shoot for an ad campaign for Old Milwaukee beer in the mid-1960s.

I lean in toward Casey in a professional photo Ricka commissioned after Chuck died in 1966.

Casey and me during a gathering with our families in Union Pier, Michigan, in 2008.

Casey and I make the most of a professional photo shoot in the mid-1960s. These formal sessions were an annual event for Ricka and Chuck, who had great aspirations for themselves and their sons.

Marilyn the Magician

His relative picked us up that evening in a big Mercedes, and when I asked him where the girls were, he said they would meet us over at his apartment at the Palm Bay Club. Huh. No McDonald's, apparently. We got to his bachelor pad, a sprawling modern space, and still no girls. But he did offer us a beer upon arrival.

After about 30 minutes of chitchat and another beer, the doorbell rang and our host went to greet the girls. In walked two grown women: a stunning brunette in a glowing purple dress down to her knees, and a tall, athletic blonde in a white jumpsuit and high heels that made her look like an Amazon. The ladies introduced themselves: Marilyn was the statuesque blonde and Alyson was the cute brunette. Frederick was the host, so he chose Alyson.

I was seated as Marilyn stepped toward me and, towering over me, asked what I wanted to do.

"I don't know," I said, my voice and body quivering.

"Where can we go?" she asked our host.

Frederick had already disappeared with Alyson into a room off the kitchen. The host guided us into a guest bedroom and, as he shut the door, said, "Have fun, kids."

I sat on the bed looking up at Marilyn. In about two seconds, she stepped out of her high heels. Then lifting one shoulder of her jumpsuit, she stepped out of that, too. Before me stood a stunning naked woman in her 20s, body fully formed but not plump, pubic hair noticeably darker than her blonde page-boy haircut.

"What do you like to do?" she asked me.

"Nothing," I said meekly. "I do nothing. I don't know how to do anything."

She sat down to my right and suggested I take off my clothes. I told her I was nervous. She said everything would be okay; she wanted to be nice to me and make me feel good. So, I took off everything except my white briefs (luckily, I was wearing a good pair that night) and sat down next to her.

"Aren't you going to take off your underpants?" she asked.

I said I wasn't sure.

"I think you should," she said.

I removed the underwear and sat back down next to her. She told me to lie back, shut my eyes, and try to relax. As I did, she took my emerging manhood into her mouth, and in less than a minute I had the first ejaculation of my life … and it was explosive. My whole body shook with ecstasy. I could feel a tingling in all parts of my skin, like when I got stung by that hornet last time I was in Florida, but so much better.

Giddy, I lay on my side on the bed as Marilyn went to the bathroom, spat out what was in her mouth, and brushed her teeth. She came back and lay next to me on the bed, and we talked. She said I was nicer than most of the men she met and told me she made enough money to own a fur coat and a pink Cadillac. After a few minutes, she asked if I wanted to try something else. I said sure.

Then she did what seemed like a magic trick. Placing a rubber on her lips and lowering herself into my crotch, she fit the plastic balloon onto my resurgent manhood. She rolled on her back and pulled me on top of her. She told me to put myself inside her, but she was much bigger than me, and as she gyrated her stomach and her hips upward it had a trampoline effect, bouncing me into the sky, so I never penetrated her. After a few minutes of this failed silliness, she stopped trying to excite me. We rolled onto our sides, facing each other, and just kept talking.

She told me she was from a small town out West. She liked what she did, but hoped one day to settle down and have a family. I told her I thought she'd make a great mom. After nearly an hour, she said, "I like you. Let's try that first thing again." And like a well-oiled machine, we were done in less than a minute and she was back in the bathroom brushing her teeth. I felt bad about her having to brush her teeth, and I told her so. "It's okay," she said. "You taste sweeter than the other guys."

At that point, our host knocked on the door and told us we needed to get dressed and come back out into the kitchen. I told Marilyn I liked her and asked if I could see her again if I came back to Miami. She said sure and wrote her name and number on the inside of a book of Palm Bay Club matches. I'd cherish THAT souvenir from Florida.

As we stepped back into the kitchen, my face was red from exhilaration and mild embarrassment. Our host asked me how she was, and I said FANTASTIC. He then asked Frederick how Alyson was, but he was less enthusiastic. "She bit me," Frederick said. "You shouldn't pay her."

The next few days were a blur as I relived my hour with Marilyn over and over in my head. I returned to Chicago feeling more grown up, more confident. As I went to sleep that first night back at the Majewskis, tucked up once again in my third floor dungeon, I thought about how remarkable the world could be. In one week, I'd gone from never having had an orgasm and being terrified of girls, to leapfrogging over all my classmates (and maybe even some Majewski boys) and having a sexual experience with a grown woman. *Darlene*, I thought as I drifted off to sleep, *you will not stop me.*

Sticky Fingers

One weekend evening, during one of the typical Majewski drunk fests, I slipped away into Lincoln Park for a walk with Amy Joseph. Amy was from Evanston, a suburb just to the north, and though she was only a year older than me, she might as well have been ten years my senior. She had the fully developed body of a gymnast, a constant tan that illuminated her freckled face, and she dated college guys. She was wise, and I felt as if I could talk with her about anything.

As we walked, I told her how unhappy Casey and I were at the Majewskis and how we felt like we were missing out on life. I worried I was losing ground that I could never make up later. I even started crying a little bit. I had the beginnings of a head cold and was feeling crummy, wallowing in my shit as only a teenager could.

She put her arm around me as we walked slowly, more like a teacher than a girlfriend, and said: "Barnaby, you are going to be okay. So is Casey. You just need to be patient, and you'll get through this. Just do your work and stay out of trouble."

At that point, we turned toward each other and she gave me a big hug as we stood under an old lamppost that lit up the heart of Lincoln Park. It was a long hug—long enough to make me think I should caress her butt or try to kiss her cheek, but that part of me that was becoming an adult resisted.

As we pulled back, I suggested we stop over on Clark Street at Sol's Pharmacy, where we could get some gum or candy. We entered Sol's—one of those small neighborhood pharmacies with the cash register in front, the pharmacy in back, and three rows of goods—and Amy stayed at the front near the candy while I ventured to the back near the cold remedies.

I noticed that Vick's VapoRub came in a small size in a little square box. I grabbed one off the shelf and stuffed it into the left front pocket of my light coat. I had stolen before, from the Woolworth's across the street (Flair felt-tip pens—I stole one whenever they came out with a new color). But I don't know what got into me to try to steal medicine.

As I got back to the front to join Amy and to look at candy, the old guy behind the counter asked me what was in my pocket. He said he could see the box through my coat. *Shit, what an idiot.*

"Give it to me right now and never come in here again, and I won't call the cops," the man said.

As Amy and I walked the few blocks back to the Majewski party, I felt stupid and embarrassed. But Amy understood. "You're not a bad person," she said. "Plus, you're the first kid ever to try to steal VapoRub. You need to work on stealing stuff that's a little more fun."

An awkward next few weeks passed as I struggled to avoid Sol's on the way to school to pick up some gum or other necessity. A few times, I was with a Majewski son and had to stay outside on the corner while he went in, which made no sense at all. After a few weeks I finally went inside after school one day and apologized to the old guy behind the counter and told him I'd never steal from Sol's again. He said he'd give me another chance.

Woolworth's, however, was not part of my agreement—its Flair pen supply would continue to be a little short.

1975

IN SOPHOMORE YEAR, I STARTED to grow beyond five feet tall. Things were looking up. I was the starting right wing on the junior varsity soccer team, and the starting second baseman on the baseball team. I laundered my own uniforms so that Darlene couldn't turn them into that Majewski all-color-wash gray. Casey excelled in soccer, basketball, and baseball, and I was proud and sometimes jealous of his achievements.

Despite the confinement of the Majewski household, Casey managed to have two serious girlfriends in high school. He was the master of slipping out at night and never getting caught. He even fooled me. I admired his courage and wondered why I didn't sneak out too (except my rooftop forays, of course.) It wasn't my style I guess ... or maybe I didn't have the passion to take the risk. I played the inside game, trying to make peace so that I could occasionally earn a privilege. Casey had declared war, and he couldn't wait to get out.

He and Darlene barely talked. She looked for any little inconsistency in anything he said or did so she could ground him for an extended stretch. The smallest misstatement or misstep would mean a week or more of solitary confinement in the Dinges Prison. The chores kept up and the dogs just wouldn't die.

Tango's Last Bite

Tango, the Alaskan Malamute, had become a complete terror and was biting people daily, including me. Imagine that! I'm walking this nasty fat-ass bitch and she's biting me for no reason. I'd had enough.

On a winter evening, I walked Tango to Lincoln Park, which was a struggle because Darlene fed her so much. The lagoon in the park had frozen over, and I walked Tango out onto the ice, which wasn't her favorite thing (despite her Arctic lineage). I held the long leather leash and started sprinting out onto the ice, dragging Tango behind me. She trotted slowly to keep up. When I got to full speed, I swung the leash around me and sent Tango careening out onto the ice. She spun slowly around, and when her legs couldn't support her anymore, she crashed stomach first onto the ice and spun a few more times until she came to a stop.

She lay on the ice whimpering for a few seconds as I stood over her. "Don't ever fucking bite me again, Tango, you bitch," I taunted her.

It was a slow walk home, but Tango never bit me again, and she steered clear of me in the house.

Casey vs. Darlene

Casey got bolder as he got closer to graduating and getting out of the house. One Saturday, he said he was going to the dance at Parker School. I went to that dance, too, but due to my 9:00 pm, curfew I was usually leaving by the time many people were arriving. At about 8:30 that night, Darlene and Alan, who were supposed to be going out to dinner, showed up unannounced at the dance, which parents never did. Darlene was looking for Casey … who was blocks away at his girlfriend's townhouse.

Darlene confronted me and asked where Casey was. I said I hadn't seen him. Then, as she turned to talk with some teachers who were chaperoning, I snuck out of the lunchroom into the alley and sprinted to his girlfriend's house. After much loud knocking, Casey and his girlfriend came to the door, barely clothed, and I warned them of the crisis underway in the Parker lunchroom.

I ran back to school and, sweating, tried to delay Darlene's exit. A few minutes later, Casey and his girlfriend arrived, and in an awkward exchange, said hello to the Majewskis.

"Something's not kosher here," Darlene said. "You boys have been sneaking around and lying to me. Casey, you are grounded for the rest of senior year. Barnaby, you will have a nine o'clock curfew for all of high school." As Casey and I stood there in stunned silence, Darlene's head continued to rock slowly side to side, like a large bell that had just been rung. The silence of her stare chilled our collective spines.

But Casey could see the end. He was a senior, and he would be graduating in 1975 and going to college. Observing my brother research, plan, and plot his college pursuit was to see Casey at his best: focused, meticulous, driven. When he graduated high school and got his freedom, he was not going to fuck it up. He would find the perfect place and never look back. I saw him pouring over college almanacs for days, making notes, and dog-earring pages. I knew not to "Och out" and distract him. I was witnessing a genius at work.

As kids we always talked about going to Michigan State, since Mom, Dad, Hans and Doreen all had history there, but MSU didn't even make it onto Casey's list. After all his note taking and analyzing and anal stressing came the big reveal … Wesleyan University in Middletown, Connecticut.

"Why Wesleyan?" I asked. "What the hell even is Wesleyan?"

I expected an answer like "good soccer program" or "coolest school you've never heard of," but what I got was "aid-blind admission."

What the hell was aid-blind admission? And why would that determine where you would want to go to college?

"Admissions pick the class they want and the college figures out the financial aid afterwards," Casey said thoughtfully. "It creates a community based on merit, not connections. It's very progressive."

I knew then my brother had his future all figured out, and I could worry about him a little less. He applied early and got accepted. I was happy for Casey, but I'd miss him when he left Chicago. And though we always had a different approach to surviving at the Majewskis, we always stuck together and supported each other through every ordeal. Soon I'd be navigating alone.

Casey was selected by his class to give the commencement address at graduation from Parker. He delivered a very serious talk about sustainability—a very adult topic for an 18-year-old. One might have thought that a young man who got good grades, was an excellent high school athlete, and who got into a good college would bring pride to his family. But Casey got none of those accolades.

The next day, right after his high school graduation, he packed up a few things and entered the Majewski kitchen around lunchtime where Darlene was sitting alone. They looked at each other from across a large table as Casey told her: "It's time for me to move on."

Darlene's one-word response was "good."

And with that Casey's seven-year stay at the Majewski house abruptly ended, and he never saw the five of them ever again. He worked for three months as a lifeguard at a swimming pool in

Sandburg Village near Chicago's Old Town neighborhood and went to live with the family of one of his soccer teammates. Then, in late summer, he drove to college in a 1971 VW bug, teaching himself to drive as he covered the 900 miles alone.

Mit Sanford

The summer before my junior year in high school, I spent as many days as possible with Mit Sanford. Everyone should have a friend like Mit. A libertarian before that term became popular, Mit was open to trying anything. He was smart and athletic and had a wry sense of humor that made him seem like a walking *New Yorker* cartoon.

Every summer day, Mit's mom, Holly, gave him $5 and told him to get out of the house and find something to do (except get arrested or do drugs). Five dollars in 1975 was serious coin, plenty for two kids to go to a Chicago Cubs game at Wrigley Field, or go to a Bruce Lee movie if it rained. Sometimes we would hit the drugstore to buy some plastic models of old cars or airplanes and buy some model glue and bright paint. We would usually get bored with such intricate projects in less than 30 minutes, and resort to either sniffing the glue until we got dizzy or stepping out into alley and smashing the little paint vials against the wall. We authored some of the earliest street art on record.

One day at the drugstore, we saw a big kid named Hondo who was memorable because he'd flunked a couple of grades at Nettlehorst, the neighborhood public school, and everyone was afraid of him. He was the size of a grown man, but he was in ninth grade. We saw him buy six tubes of model glue, but no model. As Hondo left the store with his glue in a small brown paper bag, I suggested we follow from a safe distance to see where he was going with that suspicious glue supply. He exited the store and headed east on Fullerton toward the lake and Lincoln Park. Hondo moved in a slow, lumbering way that reminded me of a bored gorilla at the zoo.

Once he got into the park, he kneeled down in a shady area and picked up a thick stick. Mit and I were spying on him from behind a tree about 100 feet away, and we watched him dig a small hole in the dirt and stared down dumbly into it for a minute. Then he took the six glue tubes out and emptied them into the bag, which he then held up to his nose, keeping it there for about a minute. He then keeled over onto his side for a minute. Reviving himself, he gently folded up the brown paper bag, dropped it into the hole, and covered it up with dirt. After a few minutes, he got up and walked back out of the park.

"Hondo is one scary dude," I said to Mit, who nodded. "But I think we need to save him."

When we were sure Hondo was long gone from the park, we sprinted over to his hole, dug up his deadly treasure, and deposited it in a Chicago Park District garbage can.

"He's going to be super pissed when he comes back to that hole and finds his stash is gone," Mit said.

"You're right," I agreed. "Let's leave him a note."

So, we went into the park office by the lagoon to borrow a pen and paper. We wrote "SOMEBODY LOVES YOU!" We folded up the paper and then buried it in Hondo's hole. For weeks, we lived with the quiet fear that Hondo would somehow find out what we did and come kill us. But the fear served as a reminder of one of the best things we ever did for a fellow human being.

Mit was always doing interesting things, and sometimes he brought me along. On one occasion, his father, Buzzy—a hard-drinking entrepreneur with a full head of oiled red hair—bought three tickets to the college All-American game. The game was at Soldier Field, where the Chicago Bears played on an AstroTurf field laid over concrete in a stadium built in 1924 for track and field. The game featured the previous year's Super Bowl Champions, the Pittsburgh Steelers, playing a team of college all-stars.

Since I rarely got out at night to see a sporting event, I was excited to join Mit and his dad. But in the second quarter of the game, the heavens opened and rain fell so hard it was pouring down the aisles of the stadium as if we were at a water park. The game was cancelled at halftime, and we slogged out of the stadium and through Grant Park until we found a Yellow Checker Cab being driven by a middle-aged man with very dark skin. We got into the cab, relieved to be out of the driving rain, but traffic was at a standstill on Lake Shore Drive. Then, out of the blue, Mr. Sanford asked: "Nigger, do you even know how to drive?"

I caught a glimpse of Mit, whose expression indicated discomfort but not surprise.

"What kind of nigger are you?" Buzzy Sanford continued. "Are you the kind of nigger who doesn't give a shit and who isn't very good at his job?"

This went on to the point when I would not have been surprised if the driver turned around and shot the three of us with a handgun. After a few more minutes of going nowhere, Mit's dad tossed a few dollar bills at the cabbie and said, "Thanks for nothing, nigger." We got out of the cab and back into the rain. We walked in silence for a long time until we got to Michigan Avenue, where we hailed a cab with a white driver. Mit and I never talked about that night, but I felt sorry that black man had to listen to that abuse. I took small comfort in feeling that I'd witnessed a person being treated much worse than Darlene ever treated me.

Book Club of One

I was never a great reader, but that didn't mean I didn't like to read books and feel their grand impact. I read three short books growing up that spoke to my soul. I believed if all kids could read them and absorb their message, they could succeed.

The first was a book of Horatio Alger stories, of which I especially enjoyed "Mark the Match Boy." These stories were incredibly simple and captured the essence of the American Dream. They told the tale of a poor orphan boy growing up on the streets of New York City during the Depression. Through hard work, saving his earnings, and a little luck, the boy goes from selling matchbooks on street corners with his clothes in tatters, to getting better jobs and a better wardrobe. Despite his hardships, he grows up to be a success and have a happy life. "Mark the Match Boy" inspired me to believe. I needed to know that success was possible. And even though I found the stories silly and predictable, they gave me hope. The lessons were: Do something good today. Do something better tomorrow. Keep doing that and you will get ahead.

The next book was *The Autobiography of Benjamin Franklin*. It was probably the first self-help book written in the United States. In it, Franklin talks about how he broke the day into 15-minute sections. He planned each day something like this: Wake up, 15 minutes for personal hygiene, 15 minutes for newspaper reading, 15 minutes of light eating, 15 minutes of walking, and so on until he turned in for the night. This book made me conscious of time and its possibilities and how every day could be managed to guarantee personal progress. His book includes helpful advice, such as: "Eat not to dullness, drink not to elevation," half of which I understood. Elevation seemed like a worthy pursuit.

And the final book in the trio was *The Autobiography of*

Malcolm X. That was probably my favorite book because it told the story of how an angry black kid from Detroit who, through intelligence and a passionate spirit, evolved into a great leader. Though he was black and I was not, Malcolm's voice spoke to me, instilling a sense of purpose: Don't be defeated. Fight on. Don't be cynical. Things can change for the better. Go get what's yours.

1976

I'd hoped Darlene would begin to cut me some slack after Casey departed for college. I was entering my junior year at Parker. My grades were good. I was starting right wing on the varsity soccer team. I had now grown to 5'5", and I'd been elected the previous year to be the student representative to the lunchroom, which was a surprisingly influential position at Parker (and I had big plans to use it to my advantage).

My whole approach the prior eight years had been to try to make peace with Darlene, to appease her demons long enough to be allowed to do some basic things. Mine had not been an "every day is war" posture like Casey. I just wanted to get along so that I could get out of the house, but Darlene always needed a target for her ire. No wonder her kids were relieved when we arrived; we took the target off their backs.

Once Casey went off to Wesleyan, he and I started exchanging letters. Darlene, of course, intercepted his letters to me and read them while I was at school. I'd come home to her steaming mad in the kitchen. As she moved around from the sink to the stove in a rare moment of movement, her head bobbing slightly, she called Casey a "sex fiend and a junkie."

Casey's letters to me were very honest. In 1976, college students across America were partaking in a fair amount of sex, drugs, and rock and roll … and my brother was typical in that way. He also told me about his classes, campus life, playing freshman soccer at Wesleyan, and having a radio show in the middle of the night.

Darlene didn't care about those details, though. She believed we Dinges boys were degenerates, and since I looked a bit like my older brother, I must share his tendencies. I was, however, becoming my own guy. I stopped playing the dumb card and dice games with Darlene because they didn't seem to pay off and I didn't have time for such silliness anymore.

Early in the school year, a first-year girl named Lindsay caught my eye. She had long brown hair, dark brown eyes, and a nifty body combination of a small butt and large breasts. She dressed casually in Levi's corduroy jeans and wool shirts, usually brown. She was shy but approachable. We didn't talk much at school, but she lived less than a half mile north of the Majewskis, so whenever I got a free hour, I'd run over to talk with her, usually out in front of her family's two-flat on Briar Place.

We went on a few dates to pizza joints in the neighborhood, but because I had to be home by 9:00 pm—even as a junior in high school—we'd talk in her first-floor vestibule, make out beneath the crystal chandelier, and then I would sprint home at 8:55, arriving drenched in sweat but exhilarated by life's first real kisses.

I liked Lindsay, but she did not appreciate or even believe my early curfew. She wanted more and figured I didn't really want to be with her. Who leaves a high school dance at 8:45 to run home to make curfew? Her breaking up with me should have been enough to urge my rebellion against Darlene and her dictatorship, but it just wasn't in me to live in daily battle. I was the comedian, not the combatant.

Nonetheless, after nearly a decade of living in the Majewski house, nearly half my life, I felt no attachment. In fact, I don't possess a single photograph of proof that I lived in that house with that family. If there was no evidence, it would be easier to forget or believe it never happened. Thankfully I was blessed with the ability to remember. How was it that Darlene, a "professional" photographer, took no family photos? Fortunately, I'd had just enough exposure to other families by age 17 to know that what I was experiencing was not normal. I would need to find love, nourishment, and family bonds elsewhere.

The Contos Family

There was a girl in my class, Maria Contos, who also lived in the neighborhood. She was from a Greek family who lived in a two-flat a block west of Clark Street near the Majewskis. Maria was a brilliant girl who was quiet in class but great in private conversation. She had a fully developed body by eighth grade, perfectly formed, and she would walk very slowly, rolling her hips side to side in a gentle rocking sway. We would often walk to and from school together, and sometimes I would linger and chat with her on the stoop in front of her brown brick three-flat.

The Contoses rented their apartment on the second floor, and I liked visiting her because her dad, Lou, who worked as a parks architect for the city, would often be in the front room smoking a cigar or drinking a Leinenkugel's beer while watching a baseball game on TV. Lou Contos had a handlebar mustache and a gruff manner that intimidated people. I found him refreshingly direct. He would often ask me what I was doing and what my plans were and how I was going to succeed.

Over many months, I developed a trust in him, so I told him about the Majewski household and all the weird and wrong things happening under that roof. He believed me and told me not to make waves and just concentrate on graduating from high school. Simple advice, but it felt good to hear it from an adult.

Maria had an older sister, Andrea, who was a taller, black-haired version of her, and even sexier. The Contos girls had dark, deep-set eyes and long straight hair down to their butts. They were so beautiful that their parents commissioned a painting of them together in bathing suits, and it hung on the wall in their dining room; it was hard for me not to stare at it.

Maria was the first girl I knew who drank coffee, and she drank it black. She also smoked cigarettes and seemed way more adult than me. We would sit and talk for hours about everything: the overdevelopment of Lincoln Park; whether Nixon was a crook; who in our class might have lost their virginity; what colleges were good; and how to live in the shadow of an older sibling. We even talked about whether we should have sex, or at least make out a bit. We decided no ... our friendship was too important, and we couldn't gossip about everybody else if we lost that. I loved Maria even more after we decided not to have sex. It felt good to know a girl who was a real friend. Maybe I was growing up after all.

Lunchroom Politics

Around this time, I was getting ambitious. I wanted things. Parker was a place guided by Chicago's richest families: the Pritzkers, Crowns, and Rosens. I didn't have their money and their family lineage, but I did have the confidence fed by my ability to compete in their world, and the charisma to attract those who didn't live in it. Deep down I felt better than the super-rich kids because I was the orphan who earned what he got. If I could overcome the loss of my parents, I could survive anything.

At the end of my sophomore year, I'd hatched a plan to get elected to a student government office so that by the end of my junior year I could run for president. One of the elected positions was Lunchroom Student Representative, and as unimpressive as that sounds, it was the perfect job for me. All the Parker kids ate lunch there, so I knew if I could improve the average lunch experience, I could get presidential election votes from all of them. I had a captive audience.

I campaigned on an aggressive platform of more varied, better tasting food and opening up the ice cream stand five days a week, not just Wednesdays. I championed the simple idea that we students were tired of eating average food and deserved a treat EVERY DAY!

I won in a landslide, though I was taken aside by some Parker administrators who shared their disappointment in me for blasting them in public without talking with them first. Lesson learned.

It didn't take much to improve the lunchroom experience, as even the administration wanted to eat better food. The lunchroom had been run like some city hall patronage operation, with bland bulk food being served in the least appealing way possible. They hired a new head of lunchroom and started to buy a variety of food from new suppliers. They even painted the lunchroom walls in bright colors and got new dishware.

The big hit was the ice cream bar, which was located right next to the cash register. I operated the thing myself, and each student who came through with their lunch was invited over for a 25-cent ice cream cone. Bulk ice cream was so cheap that I could have charged a dime for each scoop and still broken even. If a student didn't have money, I told them they could pay me later, and if it was cute girl, she could have it for FREE! I had all the favorite flavors: vanilla, chocolate, mint chocolate chip, strawberry, butter pecan, and mocha nut ... and in doing so, I was able to lay the groundwork for my grassroots presidential campaign a full year out from election day.

The Opposition

I knew getting elected president would not be easy because I would be running up against a friend and sometimes nemesis, Danny Rosen, whose older brother, Richard, was the current president. In Chicago it was tradition to pass the top job along to the next family member in line, think Richard J. Daley to Richard M. Daley as Chicago mayor. Parker was like that too. Keep it in the family … at least among the best families. I had other ideas. Danny could have all the girls and host Gatsbyesque parties at the family mansion on Hawthorn Place and star on all the sports teams, but I was going to have this.

I had known Danny since kindergarten. We became friends in middle school. He lived a few blocks away in a large second floor apartment right off Lincoln Park. He could step across Fullerton Avenue and be in the heart of Lincoln Park, and we would often gather there for pick-up baseball games where we would use large trees as both bases and foul poles. Danny had a Greek god quality about him with his wavy brown hair, blue eyes, and the build of a gifted athlete. He was good at everything … and knew it. His one weakness was perhaps humility; he had none.

One time, I was at his house when two new pairs of Levi's jeans came for him IN THE MAIL! I had never owned a new pair of jeans, let alone had my size and style arrive via the US Postal Service. His dad was independently wealthy, and would park his red Ford Mustang convertible in the alley outside their apartment so he could walk up the back stairwell right into the kitchen, where he could resume talking on the phone much of the day. Parking tickets would pile up on the front windshield of old man Rosen's Mustang each day, but he didn't care. He had that kind of money.

Danny's family always had tickets to see the Chicago Cubs, Blackhawks, and Bears games, and I would get jealous at school hearing stories about great performances by Ernie Banks or Bobbie Hull or Gayle Sayers. Occasionally, if I was lucky, I watched a game on black and white TV. Once, Danny invited me to a Blackhawks game, but it was when the Majewskis planned one of their Florida family forays, so I couldn't go. I would have given up two weeks in Florida to see the Hawks even one time. I'd never even set foot inside the venerable Chicago Stadium. In fact, I don't think my dad had ever taken me to a sporting event; I was too young before he ran out of time.

Often in class, Danny and I would position ourselves on opposite sides of the classroom and debate, leaning back in our chairs against the wall, for as long as we could until the teacher cut us off. Whether it was about Golding's *Lord of the Flies*, Orwell's *1984* or Dickens's *A Tale of Two Cities*, I would often wait until Danny had staked out a position before I would argue the opposite. I enjoyed jousting with Danny. I'm sure it annoyed him, but someone had to keep him honest and put up some semblance of resistance.

Once, in seventh grade, we were on Danny's parents' bed watching a show on their mammoth color TV when Danny surprise attacked me. He rolled me over on my back and farted on my face through his jeans and kept sitting on me until I couldn't breathe. When I came up, gasping for breath with his intense methane fart still stuck in my sinuses, I ran into the bathroom and threw up.

I wasn't always on the receiving end of aggression, though. One winter Saturday afternoon, we were out on the frozen-over Lincoln Park Lagoon. We were playing hockey in gym shoes, just the two of us, with sticks and a puck. After passing the puck for a while, Danny decided to be goalie, and we took a square garbage can from the park to use as a goal. He got down on his knees, and I skated in and shot the puck. It hit a bump in the ice, jumped up, and hit Danny in the mouth. Blood gushed out of his mouth, and we looked at the pool of blood gathering on the white-gray ice. Danny dropped his stick and ran straight home. Danny's mom took him to the dentist for emergency surgery. He needed stitches on his lip and lost two lower teeth.

I felt terrible seeing Danny bloody and in pain because of something I'd done. It was an accident, but I don't think Danny believed me, so our friendship was never quite the same after that. Darlene accused me of hurting Danny on purpose, but Mrs. Rosen forgave me and even invited me over to have a chocolate milkshake with Danny as he recuperated.

So, in junior year, when Danny and I lined up to run against each other to be student government president the following year, the conventional wisdom was that I didn't have a chance. His older brother, Richard, was the current president, and he was popular. Since Danny was a new and improved version of his brother, one had to wonder why I was even in the race. Dingeses didn't challenge Rosens, let alone beat them.

Election Landslide

Danny and I were two of the most popular kids in our class, yet we approached the election differently. He was anointed, and I felt like I had to earn it every day. I didn't mind doing it my way. While Danny was busy being Big Man on campus, I had been tending to the minions in the lunchroom for an entire year. I had a monopoly on chatting people up at the ice cream line and handing out many targeted treats. Beyond that, I'd ask kids what was important to them, and that became the basis for my campaign.

We gave our speeches in front of the entire high school (plus the eighth grade, since they would join the fray the following year). Danny went first, and he said ... something forgettable because I can't remember. I think he said something about carrying on the good work and legacy of his older brother. More Rosen!

I got up and let loose. I started by reminding them all about the better lunches, the six flavors of ice cream, and the profits I'd earned running the lunchroom, which I fed back into the school's tight budget. (There was an emerging energy crisis due to the OPEC oil embargo at the time, so the school was cutting back on hours of operation, turning off lights, and even cutting funds for student activities.) I proposed that we get administration approval for an all-night dance marathon to raise money for student activities and set a lofty goal of $2,000. I stated that just like I had improved the lunchroom experience, I would do the same for "morning exercise" (the daily all-school gathering for speakers and performances). I told the electorate: "Fewer speakers, more Flash Gordon movies!"

Then I got patriotic. I underscored the need to beat our private-school rivals to the south, The Latin Romans (where all the old-school Republican families sent their kids, since Parker was the Democrats' bastion) with greater frequency. I pledged to attend as many sports events as possible—to be their super fan—whether it was an eighth grade basketball game or girls' field hockey. I would show up and represent the Parker Colonels in full voice. The crowd cheered throughout my talk, and though it was basic, it was real. It was honest. It was me. And they loved it.

I won in a landslide, and after accepting congratulations from constituents all day long at school, I got home to a different response from Darlene. "You might be able to fool the kids at Parker, but you don't fool me," she said. "You are slacking off around the house, and I won't allow it. I won't think twice about taking you out of Parker if you don't do everything I tell you to do."

I was not surprised that, on the greatest day of my life, Darlene was trying to take away my prize. It was further proof I needed to protect what I'd earned.

A few weeks later, a Saturday, I was running around the house cleaning all four bathrooms so I could get out of the house before noon. I'd cleaned the mirrors, wiped the floors, and scrubbed the toilets; everything was minty fresh. Before I could leave the house, Darlene called me to the top of the stairs by her bedroom and told me to re-do the guest bathroom. I looked inside, inspected my work and asked what was wrong.

"Clean the toilet again," she said. "There are brown spots on the underside of the toilet seat."

We were standing face to face about two feet apart in the entrance to the bathroom, our eyes glaring at each other from the same level. I said I wasn't going to clean the toilet again. I was cleaned up and ready to go out. And with that Darlene swung her right hand up at my face. Before it could crack down on my left cheek, I raised my left hand and grabbed her forearm. Her right arm shook with her attempted force and my firm resistance. I held her arm in the air for several seconds and squeezed it hard. Before I released my grip on her quivering arm, I said, "Darlene, don't you ever fucking try to hit me again."

Without a word she went down the hall to her bedroom and slammed the door behind her. Darlene and I never discussed what happened that day, and she never raised a hand to me again. I felt a steely strength begin to emerge inside me. My days were getting better.

School Becomes Home

As president, Francis Parker increasingly became my home. I would have slept there if I could. I knew every square inch of that place, from the principal's office (I'd found a master key to the school offices on the playing field one day) to the boiler room, where I'd cleaned towels one summer. School nourished and sustained me.

I would hang out there during school holidays. My crew and I often left windows in the shop and art rooms slightly ajar, just enough so that we could sneak our grubby fingers underneath the glass and crank the windows open slowly from the outside. Parker had notoriously lax security, often with no one on campus after hours. Sometimes there was an elderly black man named James the Janitor who patrolled the halls, but it would take him five minutes to cover about 100 yards.

Sometimes we would sneak into the school for the sole purposes of annoying James for an hour or so, making noises from one end of the school to make him walk over to check it out, and then sneaking to the other end of the school and making the same noises. We were hilarious in that way.

We would often sneak into school to play floor hockey in the lunchroom. Its smooth linoleum floor was a great surface, and the built-in benches along the walls made for good checking into the boards, creating a stadium-like feel. We would use the lunch tables as goals and clear out the rest of the tables and chairs to create a perfect arena for six on six. These secret games would occur often over holidays. I especially loved it when the floor would have already been cleared to clean and wax ... we'd leave it with a thousand scuff marks from our indoor hockey sticks. I had a difficult time making eye contact with the school's small maintenance staff once school resumed after the vacation.

One holiday afternoon, Mit, Charlie, and I, plus two older kids needed to get into school to get our hockey sticks out of our gym lockers to go duel with some kids from Latin School, where an open gym was officially sanctioned. As we were cranking open a window in the shop room off the alley behind Parker (something we had done dozens of times before), a cop car came cruising down the alley. A nosy neighbor had apparently spied five teenagers "breaking into the school" and called the cops.

The other four boys were already through the window and inside the school when I climbed in and yelled "Cops!" We all sprinted in different directions, figuring we'd be harder to catch that way. I had always loved to run and felt most alive when doing so. Low to the ground, I was fast and balanced. Sprinting felt like a natural state, the activation of my animal instincts. I hoped when I died it would feel like running, running to freedom.

And that's how I felt as I made my way down Parker's linoleum floors from the north end of the building to the south. Right down the arts hallway, left down the middle-school corridor, out a secret side door, dashing along the east side of the building. I scaled a six-foot cyclone fence and launched myself onto the Clark Street sidewalk to freedom. Just then, another cop car jumped the curb and screeched to a halt right in front of me.

My escape foiled, the gig was up. A paddy wagon arrived, and the five of us, all Francis Parker students, were loaded in and taken down to the station. Once there, a grizzled old detective did his best Dennis Farina imitation and told us how we could have been shot. "If you don't straighten up," he said, "you are going down the river, and that's a place you don't want to end up."

Fuck no—we were going to college! But his point was well taken. After threatening to charge us with breaking and entering, we were given a citation for disorderly conduct and sent home in the company of our parents or guardians. Darlene had reason to be pissed ... and she was. "I told you that you and your brother are trouble. You are an embarrassment. We never should have taken you two in. I've never been so embarrassed," Darlene said.

I sat in silence for the car ride home, knowing I'd handed Darlene all the ammunition she needed to ruin the rest of my junior year. For years she had berated me for the smallest things—like calling me a liar if I said I was going to Burger King and ended up at McDonald's. She would use that "liar" label to deny me anything and everything. I couldn't be trusted.

Taking the Wheel

Darlene and Alan had paid for private driving lessons so their boys could get drivers licenses on the day of their 16th birthdays. It was a family tradition that was not afforded to Casey and me. She signed me up to take driver's education at Wells High School, a rugged public school in a gang-infested Hispanic neighborhood on the city's near-west side. I had to take a long bus ride and then run to class. It was a tense experience, but I was excited at the prospect of learning how to drive and maybe one day owning my own car and being able to go anywhere I wanted. The Majewski boys were already driving the Checker Marathon all over town, whenever they wanted.

When I received my certificate of completion for driver's ed., Darlene informed me I wouldn't be driving her car because I couldn't be trusted. This did not sit well with my friends, who saw how clearly my human rights were being violated. My friend and soccer teammate Frederick Lazar already had his own car, a sweet dark green Mercury Cougar, which had cool circular windows in the back.

Where we practiced soccer in the park, there were huge fields and surrounding parking lots. Since we were juniors, a few of us were allowed to arrive and leave in our own cars. One day after practice, Frederick asked if I wanted to practice my driving in his Cougar in the enormous and mostly empty Montrose parking lot. I said sure, and in we hopped. It felt great to be driving a car, especially one as cool as the Cougar. This was serious business, so I was locked in on driving slowly, working on my turns, parking and three-point turns—all the things I would need to know some day when I took the driver's test.

After about ten minutes of driving practice, I needed to circle back to pick up some other kids. As I pulled out of the parking lot to take a left turn, I was effectively making a U-turn near an exit ramp off Lake Shore Drive. A police car was right there as I made the turn, and I got pulled over.

Big problem. No driver's license, expired learner's permit, no ID on hand (I was in soccer shorts), illegal U-turn in traffic. Even worse, Frederick was ticketed for allowing me to drive illegally. Once again, it was back to the police station, where I was told I could have been charged with auto theft. Darlene was apoplectic and threatened to take me off the soccer team and make me quit as incoming Student Government President.

Louis Lazar, Frederick's bank president father, called Darlene to reason with her. He said Frederick and I were not bad kids, that it was an innocent mistake that could happen to anyone. He noted the situation could have been avoided if she had let me use her car to practice, and maybe got my license at the appropriate time. He offered to have the lawyer he had hired for Frederick represent me as well, since our hearing was at the same time and with the same judge.

Darlene said no. She wanted me to get the full brunt of the law. No lawyer. In fact, no defense at all. She instructed me to plead guilty to all charges and accept my punishment. So I did.

Frederick had his charges dropped. I was ordered to not drive a car until my 18th birthday.

I had lost my driving privileges before I even had them in the first place! I lost what I never had! But I still had two strong legs and the will to run wherever I needed to go. With a 9:00 pm curfew, I didn't have the need or time to drive anywhere anyway.

Surprise Party

For my 17th birthday, which had zero meaning to me, Darlene and Frederick—an unlikely duo—joined forces to host a surprise party for me at the Majewski house. This was strange because I never had a party there; it was a place to languish and I had my fun elsewhere. But Darlene was mindful that it was commonly known that Casey graduated high school and flew the Majewski coop for good with no looking back, so there was suddenly more general awareness that I had become the quail in Darlene's cross-hairs on Roslyn Place. She needed to look good.

The plan was for Darlene to host a "surprise party" and that Frederick would get 20 or so friends to each kick in $10 so he could go to his dad's bank and get me a thin gold coin for my birthday. It didn't take long for my vast network of spies and sup-porters to provide a heads up to me about what was happening. So, when I arrived "home" awkwardly that weekend afternoon, the 20 gift-givers were all lined up to the left and, starting at the farthest end of the entry room, a small blue felt box was handed my way until Frederick, the closest to me, handed it to me and said: "Happy birthday, buddy. Look inside."

As Darlene and Alan stood together to the right by the harp, I opened the box and saw the gold coin. It was cool and a nice idea, but I wasn't drawn to material things. I wanted freedom and human connection. I thanked Frederick and all the guys (no girls at this party) and then received a stiff and formal joint hug from the Majewskis. And the "party" was on.

But it wasn't a party; it was a charade and everybody attending knew it. It was an uncomfortable 90 minutes, and then everyone was gone. You can only drink so much Fanta grape and orange soda, and eat so many chips, before your body breaks down and your mind tells you to leave. I would have run out of there if I could. I was not going to pretend I lived in a happy home. Though I could act and had been in many high school plays and musicals, I couldn't be phony.

After everyone left, I asked if I could be excused to go upstairs. I was thinking about how it had been ten years since my dad had died. I was becoming a man, at least a baby version of one, and I missed him. I'm not sure I had ever felt more alone than that night. I cried myself to sleep and wished I'd never been born.

Forcing My Hand

Junior year wound down without drama. I felt lifeless and wondered how I would survive my senior year and another year at the Majewskis without my brother. He was doing great at college, excelling in his classes, and had a girlfriend whom he had met on his first day, a beautiful Jewish girl from Great Neck, Long Island who wanted to be a doctor. Casey had it going on, and he reported his success and occasional excesses thoroughly to me in detailed letters that came every two weeks.

I was looking forward that summer to being a camp counselor at Francis Parker, a step up from being the towel boy. I couldn't get away from Parker, and I didn't want to. Casey planned to come home that summer to work again as a lifeguard at the Sandburg Village apartments in Old Town. It was a sweet gig, sitting in a chair ogling high school girls and their hot moms. I was anticipating spending some time with my brother, maybe even hanging by the pool with him.

Soon after school ended for the year, I was summoned to Darlene's second-floor bedroom. She was in a robe, which was strange for mid-afternoon. She'd intercepted a recent letter from my brother, again describing parties and girls and drugs and all the things that happened on college campuses in 1976.

"Your brother is a bad influence, and I don't want you seeing him this summer," she announced.

Stunned, I asked, "What are you taking about?"

As she sat on her bed leaning back on pillows, she waved Casey's letter above her head and said: "It's all right here. I'm not going to let you become like your brother. I want you to call him up right now and tell him you will not be seeing him this summer. In fact, tell him you will not be seeing him ever again. I'm going to send you away to school, so you can forget about your senior year here, soccer and Student Government President. And I want you to call up the people at Parker Day Camp and tell them you are quitting your job."

"I haven't even started the job yet," I said. "I can't quit what I haven't started. Why are you doing this?"

"Call your brother right now. I want to hear every word you say," she instructed me.

I walked over next to Darlene and picked up the push-button phone connected to a long tangled cord. In my pocket, I had the number of a friend of Casey's where he had been staying since he got back into town. He came to the phone and I said, "Case, it's Bar. Darlene is not going to let me see you this summer while you are in town. I'm sorry."

On the other end of the phone Casey was asking questions that I didn't want to answer. He was angry, but he could tell by my voice that I was in a para-hostage situation. Something was seriously wrong. At that point, Darlene grabbed the phone from me and started screaming into the mouthpiece: "You are a fucking junky and pervert, and I'm not going to let you destroy your brother."

I could hear Casey screaming, "Fuck you, Darlene!" over and over into the phone before she slammed the phone down and hung up.

"You are not allowed to see or talk with your brother ever again," Darlene said. "Now I want you to call the head of the camp and tell him you are not working there this summer."

For a second I was frozen, but then my brain re-engaged. I told her I needed to go up to my room and get the phone number from my desk. Once I got out of her room, I leapt up the stairs, grabbed the one thing of value I could carry (my bank book showing a $452 balance), and careened down the third floor staircase by Darlene's bedroom yelling, "I'M LEAVING."

I ran down the stairs and out of the house, taking a quick left toward Clark Street. Anyone watching would have seen a boy on fire, running with terror. The combination of sprinting at full-speed and tears pouring from my eyes made me feel like a racecar driver looking through a rainy windshield. I took a left onto Clark Street and ran in the middle of the road along the white dotted line, unaware of cars and people. It was blurry, but I could see freedom.

I covered three city blocks in about two minutes. At the end of my run, out on the sidewalk in front of his friend's house, stood my brother with open arms. As we cried and held each other Casey said, "Bar, I knew you'd come."

And that was the end of my ragged run, and the start of a life I could own.

epilogue

I AM THE LUCKIEST UNLUCKY person I know. While losing my parents in childhood was a devastating, life-changing blow, throughout my youth I was also the beneficiary of exposure to healthy households where love and intellectual enrichment were exercised on a daily basis.

Chief among those families was the Farwells, my best friend Charlie's family, who invited me to live with them for my senior year of high school and then kept inviting me back for holidays and family gatherings until I became a son to Bob and Carol, and a brother to Robin, Leslie, and Charlie.

Bob and Carol knew my parents and shared their values. I showed up to live with them at 17 and told them I wanted to give them my monthly Social Security check (the one the Majewskis had been pocketing for nearing a decade), and they told me they wanted me to deposit it in my bank account and save it for college. I knew things would be different with them.

Bob and Carol showed me nothing but love, and they let me be me. They trusted me, which was probably the biggest change at the time. They had faith in me. They had expectations for me that I would make something of myself and be a positive force in their family. They kept the bar raised high, and that gave me confidence to take on life's challenges and to dream a little bit too.

I knew Carol from being around the Farwell home growing up, but Bob I got to know once I went off to college at Wesleyan University in 1977. During the summers in college I would come home to Chicago to work construction jobs, and Bob, who worked as an executive director in the nonprofit sector, would be home alone at the Lincoln Park apartment as the rest of the Farwells were up in Door County, Wisconsin, at the lakeside family cabin.

Bob and I would strip down to undies and t-shirts, and over a dinner of hot dogs, Spaghetti O's, and Special Export beer, we would talk about the world—long talks about any topic that went on for two hours. While my friends were off drinking pitchers of beer around town, I was soaking up Bob's wisdom.

Bob Farwell was the smartest person I ever met; he knew how to ask questions in a way that would lead you to a higher understanding of everything. He taught me how to connect one idea to another, and then to another ... and to me that is the true sign of human intelligence. Smart people connect ideas and find new and clever ways to do so.

Bob could also boil things down to their core essence. I remember considering careers in education, journalism, and politics after I got out of college, and Bob simply said: "You need to thrash about a bit, and then you'll figure it out." Best advice I ever got, and I pass it along to young people whenever I can. I loved the Farwells so much that when I became a father in 1990, my son's name became Cooper Farwell Dinges. And when Hayden was born in 1992, he got the middle name Leonhardt to carry on that part of the family.

Getting divorced in 2000 felt like a death blow, but with the new millennium, I thought I'd give myself a shot at happiness and finally come to grips with the pain and guilt I felt for losing my parents. I needed to learn that loss is a part of life ... but not all losses are fatal. Some losses are necessary, even good. Shed your load. Move forward. Make progress. Become stronger.

The bonus for me was to be there for my sons. I was not going to have them grow up without a dad. No way. I was going to be there for them, to watch them grow up in a way my dad never got to experience. I didn't want my kids to have the pain and loneliness I had. I was not going to give in to depression and death. I was going to live. I was going to BE PRESENT.

There's another "person" I need to thank … Francis W. Parker School in Chicago. For me, Parker was a living creature that sustained me. The school was steeped in humanity. Of all the decisions my parents made in their time together, none was wiser than sending Casey and me to FWP in the early 1960s.

Parker was always a different kind of place. For starters, every day the entire school would gather in the auditorium for something called "Morning Exercise." The exercise involved no sweating; it was intellectual—an all-school presentation or conversation. But what I remember most, and what was drilled into the minds of all Parker students, were the words in big block letters above the auditorium stage:

> ## "A school should be a model home, a complete community, an embryonic democracy."

And that's exactly was Parker was for me. It comforted me like the home I needed. I knew everybody at the school, and they knew me. I felt like I mattered, my voice and my person mattered. It helped that the school always seemed open and was never locked up or secured. The school was always alive … and I felt energized there. There were ratty old couches in the school entryway, known as The Alcove, where students could spend hours doing whatever. Mostly talking and challenging each other. When a Ping-Pong table appeared in The Alcove, it was there for months before school administrators deemed it a noisy distraction and the competitive matches were leading to too many fist fights.

Parker was a laboratory for ideas and language, where students were encouraged to express themselves with complete candor. Teachers were like parents (the good kind). The place was competitive as hell, but everybody got a chance to try things. That's why over the years so many great writers (Jonathan Alter, David Mamet) and actors (Jennifer Beals, Anne Heche, Amy Landecker, Billy Zane) have emanated from Parker.

This memoir ends in 1976 because that's when my life became normal, unexceptional, livable. I've done all the things I'm sure my parents would have wanted me to do, including watching two sons grow up to be impressive young men. I've seen much of the world and had challenging and rewarding careers. I've experienced deep and lasting love. Through it all, I am thankful for having seven memorable and formative years with my parents, Ricka and Chuck—and for my ragged run, which has been memorable as hell.

about the
author

BARNABY LEONHARDT DINGES has been writing professionally for nearly 40 years and has authored features for the *Peoria Journal Star*, *Berkeley Gazette*, and *Contra Costa Independent*. He has also worked as an investigative journalist for *The Chicago Reporter* and, as a freelance writer, has published stories with *Chicago* magazine, *Columbia Journalism Review*, *Chicago Sun-Times*, and *Chicago Reader*.

His varied career began as a teacher at the Francis W. Parker School in Chicago, his alma mater. He also worked for many years in Illinois politics and international public relations. Barnaby is a graduate of Wesleyan University in Middletown, Connecticut, and received an MSJ from the Medill School of Journalism at Northwestern University.

He lives in Northfield, Illinois with his wife Vicky and their famous Cairn Terrier, Emerson Boozer—aka The Coyote Wrestler. Barnaby's interests include Chicago sports (Bears, Bulls, Cubs, Hawks) and spending time with his adult sons, Cooper and Hayden. Dinges is a frequent visitor to his parents' gravesite at the historic Graceland Cemetery just north of Wrigley Field in Chicago. *Ragged Run* is his debut book.